Free Bodies and Minds Held Captive

By
Billy Yancey

Table of Contents

Dedication

To my mom and Clyde, who have never left my side. When I was at my lowest, they helped me up. When William was in the NICU at his worst, they traveled from afar, stayed, and prayed. During my divorce, they stood by me. When I went astray, they led me back. Despite all my sins, they forgave me and gifted me a Bible. To God be the glory! "Count it all joy." (James 1:2)

Acknowledgement

First and foremost, I express my gratitude to my grandparents, the late Maxie C. Robinson Sr., and Doris Robinson Griffin, for laying the foundation for our family, loved ones, and friends worldwide. They instilled in us the importance of faith, values, character, and integrity, along with commandments and rules to live by. I deeply miss my grandparents, and their legacies continuc to endure. May their souls rest in peace.

I feel incredibly fortunate to have been mentored by my uncles, Maxie Robinson Jr., and Randall Robinson, both of whom have now joined the presence of Jesus. They were pioneers who left a lasting impact on our family, friends, and the world at large.

Additionally, I extend my gratitude to my brother and sister in Christ, David and Katie Bingham. They played a crucial role in steering the ship when I was lost at sea. Their love, support, and friendship have been monumental.

I am grateful for the contributions of all mentioned individuals to the creation, writing, and completion of this book. May God bless them abundantly.

About the Author

Billy Yancey, a 55-year-old African American entrepreneur, boasts a remarkable 30-year tenure in the fitness industry. In 2005, he ventured into entrepreneurship, founding ANABO Exercise and Nutrition, a leading fitness technology company. Despite facing two divorces, two bankruptcies, and the challenges of the Covid pandemic, Billy's business thrives, making him the longest-standing African American gym owner in Virginia Beach—20 years and counting. Notably, Billy co-parents his 17-year-old son, William Jr., who, despite being born a micro preemie at 1lb-14ozs, has defied odds due to the unwavering faith of Billy and his former wife in God's grace.

Billy graduated from the United States Naval Academy in 1992. During his four years, he excelled as the starting cornerback for the varsity football team and was elected President of the Black Studies Club. Over three years, he served on the Service Selection Committee for various service academies, including the Naval Academy, Air Force Academy, West Point, and Merchant Marine Academy, operating out of Congresswoman Elaine Luria's office in Virginia Beach, VA. Billy found fulfillment in contributing to the selection process for future leaders dedicated to serving and protecting the country.

Throughout his career, Billy has impacted thousands of individuals of all ages locally and globally, spanning locations such as Aruba, Costa Rica, Iceland, Ireland, Cape Town, and Senegal, Africa.

Presently, Billy, a two-time Mr. Virginia Bodybuilding Champion

(1999, 2001), collaborates with a diverse team to develop a mobile application using machine learning, catering to all fitness levels, set to launch in January 2024. Despite his busy schedule, Billy has authored two books— "Free Bodies and Minds Held Captive," aimed at aiding young adults and older individuals in battling adversity, and "Anabo Nutrition," a step-by-step guide for achieving excellent health through a straightforward process. With ANABO, Billy is confident in delivering personalized, timed health and fitness solutions to Hampton Roads and beyond.

In addition to his ventures, Billy launched the "Billy and THE GOAT" podcast in the fall of 2022, dedicated to helping individuals overcome life's challenges, anxiety, and adversity.

Reflecting on his past, Billy recounts being one of two African American students in his graduating class at Landon School, a private college preparatory school for young men in Bethesda, MD. Despite facing prejudice and daily torment, Billy prevailed and graduated in 1987 with the esteemed honor of receiving the William Harrison Triplett Award for "team dedication, respect for opponents, and outstanding spirit in athletics." In 2018, he returned to Landon as the keynote speaker for the Chris Nelson Lecture Series, receiving a standing ovation for his "Quit or Fight" presentation. Billy has also shared his experiences at First Colonial High School in Virginia Beach, VA, and the Norfolk Christian School in Norfolk, VA.

Billy acknowledges that Landon School played a pivotal role in shaping his life. Without it, he believes his journey to the Naval Academy, service in the U.S. Navy as an Ensign, being stationed in Norfolk, VA, and ultimately becoming a father to William might not have transpired. Grateful for both fruitful and barren opportunities, Billy sees himself as a product of all his triumphs and failures.

Dear young adult,

One of the hardest aspects to convey to you is the mirage of the even "playing field." So many of you are led to believe that because you shine amongst your peers in your present setting, your current habits are enough. You believe it is all you need to be successful. You are wrong! So many are content with the status quo, average, or mediocrity, and that is fine. But understand that, too, is limiting. God did not create any of us to be less than. God created us to be the best version of ourselves in His likeness. We are here to serve.

Remember this! We can learn from every situation, occurrence, and conversation. Yes, there is always a lesson. In every lesson, there is a blessing. The lesson is the work you put in, stay in, and work through when life goes sideways. The lesson cannot be learned during an instance or scrolling social media pages. The lesson may only be understood and learned by enduring the pangs manifested over time. Every step we take is practice for the next.

"Order my steps in thy word: and let not any iniquity have dominion over me." Psalm 119:133

Sincerely,

Billy

Chapter One: The Ledge

**"But he said to me, "My grace is sufficient for you, for my
power is made perfect in weakness."
Therefore, I will boast all the more gladly about my weaknesses,
so that Christ's power may rest on me." 2 Corinthians 12:9 NIV.**

Have you ever stood with your toes straddling the ledge of a
building? Then, laying back with outstretched arms to do a back dive
to the pavement that plummets three stories below. I have.

This happened back in the summer of 1990. Today, I am still
perplexed by what happened. How did it even come to that? How did
I end up in such a dark space? What I experienced was the culmination
of a hardening of the attitude, which causes a person to cease
dreaming, seeing, thinking, and leading. It is the hardening of the
mind so that we become unteachable: we stop learning, and we stop
growing. It is called **psychosclerosis**. It is a thing. It is real. I am
authoring this book with the hopes that it will help you stay out of the
darkness, make better decisions, and live a positive, more productive
life.

It took 26 years for me to realize I tried to kill myself. It took more
than two decades for this to marinate and finally register in my mind.
I believe, in life, there are times when we have done things
unknowingly, not recognizing the gravity of our actions, oblivious of
consequences had our intentions come to fruition.

That is what happened to me. In my drunken state, I stood on the
third-story balcony of a condominium while my friend J.C. clung
desperately to me to save my life while I tried to take it. But God said
no, not yet.

How did I get to *that point*? If I loved me so much and all that I had become, what could drive me to **the ledge**? What happened on July 13, 1991?

Captain Redden: "State your name, midshipman candidate"

Me: Midshipman Candidate William Yancey, sir.

Captain Redden: Midshipman Candidate Yancey, per Nav Regulations 2.921968ALPHA, it is required that you have a grade point average no lower than 2.0. First trimester you had a 1.4. Now, halfway through the second trimester, things have not improved. Explain yourself, midshipman candidate!"

Me: Sir, no excuse, sir.

Me: Don't give me that crap, Yancey. What is the problem?

Me: Captain Redden, I have been working hard, sir. I get extra help. Ms. Ruffin, my physics teacher, says I am doing a lot better. That is my hardest subject, sir.

Captain Redden: That is good, Mr. Yancey. Now, what about the rest of your classes???

Me: No excuse, sir.

***Captain Redden: (With a long stare):* Step outside, Mr. Yancey, so the board can make a decision.**

They called me back in for the decision.

Captain Redden: Midshipman Candidate Yancey, you have been dismissed from the United States Naval Academy Preparatory School, NETC Newport, Rhode Island. Per Nav Regulations 2.921968ALPHA, you must have a grade point average no lower than 2.0 in order to attend the United States Naval Academy. You have a 1.4. We acknowledge your hard work and improvement recognized by your instructors; HOWEVER, the board does not believe you will turn this around in time. You have two choices: 1) Go home immediately, or 2) Stay here and prove us wrong by the end of this trimester. Work your

tail off, graduate from here, and go on to the Naval Academy. The choice is yours, Mr. Yancey. Good luck.

Dead silence. I stood at attention while a long table of civilians, lieutenants, majors, and captains stared at me. I was speechless. "You're dismissed, Mr. Yancey," affirmed Captain Redden.

I walked out dejected. I thought, **"NOW WHAT?!"** I only had one option, and it was *not* to go home and face my mom. No way. I made the decision to stay and fight. Digging my way out of a 1.4 GPA halfway through the school year would not be easy. Up until that point in my life, dodging that bullet was my toughest challenge. If academics were my only obstacle, then it would not have been so bad.

But that was not the case. Aside from endless responsibilities as a midshipman candidate, room and uniform inspections, platoon and company duties, posting watch at a duty station, enduring practices, and workout with the football team, as well as marching tours on the Grinder - to add insult to injury, my Uncle Max was dying back home in Washington, D.C. The pressures I faced throughout my Navy days were mammoth.

On July 30, 1987, midshipman candidates from all over the country and I flew to TF Green Airport in Warwick, Rhode Island. A Navy bus was waiting to take us to the Naval Education and Training Center in Newport, RI. That is where the Naval Academy Preparatory School (NAPS) is located. Having absolutely no idea what to expect, we were all anxiously quiet as we rode over the Newport Bridge. We could see NAPS and the rest of the training center as we reached the top of the bridge.

Captain Redden, the director of training, was waiting for us outside in the parking lot. He and a lieutenant had a check-in table set up about two hundred feet from our barracks. Captain Redden was confident and soft-spoken. He was not big in stature but stood with his presence. "Work hard, play hard" was his motto. "Welcome to NAPS, midshipman candidates. Where are you all from?" Gleefully, we each shared our hometowns and how eager we all were to get started. He gave us a few details and motioned us to the barracks doors behind him, where there were three hundred two-person rooms. Captain Redden continued, "After stowing your gear in your rooms, we will all meet as a group later. Your platoon commanders will tell you everything you need to know." If that was not a play on words, then I don't know what was!

It was not until months later that I realized that the intake desk was intentionally positioned a great distance away from the barracks. They did not want us to hear all the screaming going on inside. It was CRAZY. As soon as we walked through the barracks doors, *it was on*! This angry guy in fatigues ran up to me out of control yelling:

WHY ARE YOU WALKING, MISTER!

DON'T EYEBALL ME, SON!

GET YOUR EYES IN THE BOAT!

AREN'T YOU SUPPOSED TO GREET ME WHEN YOU PASS ME?

HURRY UP AND STOW YOUR GEAR IN YOUR ROOM, MIDSHIPMAN CANDIDATE!

HURRY BACK! I'M WAITINGGGGGG!

So, this was the day for which I could not wait?

The platoon commanders shattered my expectations. The closest I ever came to anything like that was two-a-day football practices in high school, where I got to go home and hang out every night. Not here. When you are told ahead of time that bootcamp is mostly a mind game, one cannot fully understand the truth of that statement until you are in *the game*. The Dean of Academics said it best when all 250 of us midshipman candidates were seated in a huge auditorium. "Look to your left. Look to your right. Look in front of you and behind you. That person will not be here for graduation." Attrition was like a virus. I WAS SCARED OUT OF MY MIND.

There were three companies with two platoons in each. I was in third company, second platoon. We called ourselves The Zoo, 3-2 Zoo. The nickname was perfect. During the indoctrination period, one of the keys to survival was circumventing our superiors. The less we saw them, the better. They were first class (seniors) from the Naval Academy who volunteered to make our lives a living hell. For the life of me, I could not understand who in their right mind would want to waste part of their summer training a bunch of teenagers. Wake up at O-DARK-THIRTY, throw a metal trash can down the center of our passageway, kick our doors in, scream, **"IT'S A FINE NAVY DAY,"** take us on a long run, then PT (physical training) the crap out of us. JOY.

It was an interesting summer. Many of us were petrified. Remember, one of the keys to survival was circumventing interaction with our superiors. As in, do not get caught outside your room by a superior. At all costs, avoid being questioned, inspected, ridiculed, and screamed at. That would be dreadful. If one suffered, then we all suffered. When a classmate was caught or ambushed by one or more superiors, the rest of their company mates were supposed to come and support them, aka join in the fun and suffer as a team. It just kept getting better.

Our code was plain and simple: **STAY IN YOUR ROOM.** They cannot get you if they do not see you.

One kid was so scared to come out of his room that he took a crap in his trash can. He could not face the possibility of being caught outside of his room. He was not the only one making a head call in his room. Countless were peeing out of their windows. Crazy, right?

Speaking of crazy. Remember, this is in the middle of the summer. One night, they ordered our entire platoon to put on both pairs of our heavyweight hooded sweatsuits. They called it "DOUBLE BANANA GEAR" because they were bright yellow. They ordered us into the laundry room. Somehow, the dryers were turned on and stayed on, pumping out heat with the dryer doors still open. Thirty-something bodies getting PT'd while wearing double-banana gear in a heated laundry room with our hoodies tied so only our noses peeked through. It got REAL HOT REAL FAST.

The dean was spot on. My classmates were disappearing left and right. Like me, many were dismissed from the academic board, while others just quit because they had had enough. As fate would have it, I made it. But it was far from easy. The responsibilities that come with being a student-athlete seemed insurmountable at times. Despite my talents on the football field, combined with my will and determination to defy the taunts and threats strewn by our superiors, I was compelled to embrace the *consequences* of not living up to the standards required of a student-athlete (1.4). Consequences will break you or make you, period. If embraced properly, consequences can inspire us and launch us on an amazing trajectory. Consequently, pun intended consequences can ruin us.

I refused to ruin myself, especially by my own recklessness. The reason that I was failing was not due to a lack of intellect. I am smart and always have been. I graduated from one of the premier private schools in Bethesda, Maryland: Landon School. The reason that I had a 1.4 GPA and was failing out of the Naval Academy Preparatory School is because I was lazy. Sure, I was attentive in class and got extra help afterward from my teachers, but I WAS NOT STUDYING. I was skimming over lessons, so I could go hang out in town. There were times when I did not even skim the lesson. I just skipped reading the homework and tried to make up for it in class. FAIL. That may work for some, but it certainly does not work for me. To make matters worse, our football coach, Coach Drake, found out about my academic struggles. So, not only did I get reprimanded in class, but I was chewed out numerous times in the locker room, the weight room, and on the football field.

After my academic board, everything changed. Everything. I averaged between a 2.8-3.0 GPA. How? I stopped being lazy and focused on my goal: graduate from the United States Naval Academy, become a Naval Officer, and serve my country. That required graduating from NAPS first, which meant eliminating partying and reckless behaviors, then adopting and infusing sound study habits. A major motivator was not letting my mom down. She was completely unaware of my academic board and findings. As far as I was concerned, she would never find out. The last person I wanted to contend with regarding poor grades and laziness was my mom. No way. My mom did not play. I straightened right up.

Coach Drake was all over me every day. I did not mention this earlier, but Captain Redden, the gentleman who recommended my separation from NAPS, well, he was also the NAPS Football Team Liaison. Yep. I was 100% ingrained in my studies. My teammates even started calling me a "nerd" and "brown noser" because I stopped hanging out. Onto Annapolis!

Everything about plebe summer at the United States Naval Academy is hard: being dropped off by your parents on I-Day, getting all your hair cut off, eating breakfast, lunch, and dinner in King Hall while sitting at attention, chopping up and down the steps and passageways being harassed by upper-class, sleeping and thinking about what's happened and what will happen next, uniform and room inspections, formations, chow calls, sweating before you get in the shower, sweating while you're in the shower, sweating when you get out of the shower, EVERYTHING! This was normalcy. What was not normal was when one of our classmates decided to take his own life. My company, 8th Company, was on 5-3, which was in the fifth wing, on the third deck. Our fallen classmate's company was in the fifth wing, on the fourth deck, the floor right above us. He was on the top floor. He jumped!

When that happened, although it was only hours, everything STOPPED. Plebe Summer stopped. Hazing stopped. Upper-class screaming at us and referring to us as the "lowest of the low" stopped. Chopping up and down the halls stopped. It was like we were flying in an aircraft with nowhere to land. Not increasing or decreasing in altitude, we were in a holding pattern. I remember sitting out in the hallway with my classmates and a few of our upper-class discussing what just happened. No yelling, screaming, none of that. Strange. Look, when you have been hollered at by someone who is in your face, nose to nose, for weeks, and no matter what you say or do, IT IS ALL WRONG, and then suddenly they are sitting down next to you having a cordial, two-way conversation, it is a bit unnerving. And then, the next morning, "REVEILLE! REVEILLE! ALL HANDS HEAVE UP AND TRUCE OUT!" Back to the grind. Everything was hard.

So, how did I get to the ledge 3 years later? Well, after 10 lemon drops, which was ten shots of 151 Vodka with a lemon wedge and a pinch of sugar, I jumped into my car with my friend, JC, to search for our three girlfriends who got lost while running an errand. I lost a shouting match with a pedestrian who claimed I tried to run him down in the middle of the street. He was half right. I was closer to the sidewalk when I just missed him. I was nowhere near the middle of the street. He called the police, and they pulled me over a few minutes later as I approached our condominium with our girlfriends in tow.

Somehow, I got off with just a reckless driving ticket. The police officers gave my car keys to JC and made us walk back to the condo. When we finally reached the 3rd floor, I wanted another drink, but mysteriously, all the alcohol had disappeared. I was pissed. I LOST IT! I screamed at my girlfriend, her girlfriends, and then my friend. Next thing you know, I am out on the ledge of the balcony, with my back to the parking lot. That is what happened. Me attempting to jump to my death like my classmate was no coincidence.

*It has been my experience that one of the easiest places for you to get into that does not require a key is **YOUR HEAD**. Likewise, one of the hardest places to get out of that does not require a key is **YOUR HEAD**.* Left to our own devices, we can create a living hell inside our heads for pennies on the dollar. I combatted nefarious habits inside of my head and a foolhardy mindset for years.

I would replay, rewind, and replay that afternoon over and over in my head countless times. JC and I talked about it sparingly over the years, but each time, it was as real as when it happened. "JC, how was that even possible, man?" "Billy, I was holding onto you as tight as I could! You laid back away from me, and suddenly, you were gone. I could not hold you anymore. I just yelled and slammed my hands against my face. I looked down, expecting to see you sprawled out on the cement. Somehow, you were standing with both feet on the railing of the floor below us. The railing, bro! On the railing!"

Somehow, some way, I dodged death. Just thinking about it makes me shudder. This happened in 1990. I was 22 years old. I am 55 today. 33 years of life's experiences and more would have vanished in an instant! No commissioning, no Surface Warfare Officers School, no marriage, no William, no 2x Mr. Virginia, no ANABO, no a lot of things. Wow!

I have made a plethora of mistakes along the way. I encourage you to minimize yours. Although infinite lessons can be taught to us, it seems the most valuable and most meaningful are the ones that are experienced. Sometimes, it takes going through the fire, feeling the heat, getting burned, and even scorched to learn and embrace the lesson.

I am a firm believer in the fact that there are no coincidences. All that I went through was meaningful, purposeful, and meant for me only. No one else. I have no regrets. I have learned so much from my experiences, am grateful for all of them, and am still learning. Learning never stops. We can learn a lesson from every experience and everyone. That includes those we could not care less about and even those who do not like us, especially them. Some call them enemies. I call them frenemies. What we do with the lesson is up to us.

Personally, as we all have, I had a lot going on leading up to *the ledge*; one of my favorite uncles died, my parents' divorce was unsettling, my relationship with my father was erratic, my girlfriend and I were on the rocks, our football team was led by a new coaching staff, I despised my new defensive backs coach, I was eventually demoted from being the starting cornerback on the football team, one of our teammates, who was a fellow defensive back, mysteriously *hung himself,* my mom was going through a rough patch, I was charged with a 5000-degree offense (the highest is 6000/expulsion) for driving my car on campus to help a perspective Navy football recruit, docking me of 45 days of liberty, even though I had permission from the coaching staff. A lot happened. THERE WAS A LOT GOING ON IN MY HEAD.

Things happen, yes. But, when they happen, good or bad, do you react, respond, or remain? There is a difference. Unfortunately, I wasted time reacting to adversities, instead of responding or doing nothing at all. Reacting involves little to no thought. Reacting begets self-retribution, which can be problematic. When we respond, thinking is usually involved, and we tend to make better decisions. If we do nothing or remain idle, then the likelihood of making a fool out of oneself diminishes greatly! Take heed. Sometimes, doing or saying nothing speaks the loudest. These are attributes that I would have to practice over time.

For instance, in 1989, after losing the Army/Navy game, I went out for dinner and drinks with three of my teammates. Remember earlier when I said, "left to our own devices"? Well, here ya go. As usual, I had too much alcohol. When we pulled up to my mom's apartment in Philadelphia, I got out of my friend's car drunk with an attitude. One of the neighbors yelled, "Keep it down." at me from his window. At 1:30 am in the morning, he had every right to yell at me. Of course, I disagreed, so I REACTED. I start screaming obscenities, charging toward his apartment, telling him what I am going to do to him, and blah blah blah. Fortunately, for all parties, Big Mike, one of my best friends and offensive linemen, grabbed me and insisted on me walking in the opposite direction, to my mom's apartment. Well, I did not go peacefully. I ended up ripping the entry door off its hinges, putting my fist through her wall, and blood everywhere. Had I only used one of my tools. Instead of thinking and responding or remaining, I chose to react. I made a fool out of myself.

The back story is during that time period, North Philadelphia (North Philly) was crime-ridden, and the police were notorious for using deadly force on black people during traffic stops and altercations. Although a close family friend, Kemery, explained to my mom that, "the position that Billy plays, along with how he is trained, raises him to levels on the football field that are hard to come down from when reentering society." Either way, she pleaded for me to get in the apartment. When I finally settled down, she banished me, sending me back to the hotel where our football team was staying. She was deathly afraid that the police were going to come and either hurt or kill her baby.

Moving forward, the sad news is I made numerous mistakes. The good news is I learned from those mistakes, which made me a better person. Much is gained from winning, but more can be accomplished from losing. Today, I am still making mistakes, and I am still learning. When you refuse to learn more, you stunt your growth. I am still growing. I will never get "there," but I will try forever.

I have always had a value system in my repertoire. I may have strayed from the path along the way, but I have always had tools to help me get back on track. There are times I used a hammer when a chisel was my best option. As time passes, white gloves, along with a level, have been my instruments of choice. But please do not misunderstand my smaller tool selection for weakness. My perspective, as well as my approach, is much different. If I want to get into the room, I will not come through the wall; I will walk through the door. If I cannot add to the conversation, then I keep my mouth shut.

My family raised me to be good, do good, and persevere when terrible things happened. My mom is my greatest teacher. But she did not learn these lessons on her own. Like me, she had help. We come from a lineage of good, wholesome, diligent men and women, the Robinson family. One of them is my grandfather, my mother's father, Maxie C. Robinson Sr. He is one of the cornerstones of the Robinson family value system. Maxie was a consummate husband, father, grandfather, teacher, coach, and friend. To know my grandfather was to have blessings beyond measure. He was strong-willed, resolute to a fault, and extremely competitive. He was a fierce running back in his day and an even more ferocious coach. His grit, determination, and will helped him guide several teams of young men in football, basketball, baseball, and track, where they amassed a total of ten district and ten state titles. That is twenty championships in four different sports. In 2019, posthumously I had the honor and privilege to accept his award and induction into the CIAA Hall of Fame on behalf of the Robinson family. My grandfather is legendary.

I would be remiss if I did not acknowledge the fact that I am just like my grandfather. We are both great fathers, mentors, and coaches of athletes, disciplined and have a strong faith. We also have a meticulous work ethic, work long hours, and have a great smile.

All kidding aside, for the Anabo exercise program I created, our areas of focus are core strength, muscular strength, cardiovascular, and mental toughness. Visiting family in St. Kitts a few years ago, my Uncle Randall and Aunt Hazel shared an old article written about my grandfather. While reading it, I discovered that the core values my grandfather infused into his athletes were conditioning, strength training, fundamentals, and courage. I am 100% Maxie C. Robinson Sr.

Despite the many references to myself and my family, this book is way more about you than it is about me. Going forward, I will share and discuss in detail a host of my failures, struggles, and pivotal life events, as well as how they made me feel, the actions I took, good and bad, and what tools I used to mitigate the situation…react, respond, or remain. Failures, struggles, and pivotal life events can be your springboard or your quicksand. Take your pick. Up or down.

Chapter Two: Discipline!

"For the moment, all discipline seems painful rather than pleasant, but later, it yields the peaceful fruit of righteousness to those who have been trained by it."
Hebrews 12:11 ESV

"Ok, guys, Oklahoma drill! Let's see what we got. Give me two lines facing each other, ten yards apart. Let's go! Hop to it! Line 'em up. On your back, Billy. You got the ball. You are the running back. Mike, you're tackling." As I remember it, this was one of my first football practices ever. My parents signed me up to play on the 95-lb football team. Boy, was I both nervous and excited. It was my first-time playing contact football. I mean, I played football in the street with my friends, but that was a two-hand touch. It usually turned into pushing and shoving, sometimes into a parked car or pole, but it was not tackle-football. We lived in Washington, DC. Actually, we lived in Silver Spring, MD, which is right outside of DC. Of course, we were huge Redskins fans. My family knew the late legend and starting safety, Brig Owens, well. I had the opportunity to meet and hang out with him occasionally, as well as his teammates at Redskins Football Camp in Culpepper, VA. That was incredible! Aside, of course, from having a gun pulled on me in our cabin by one of the campers. Yup, I ran back to my bunk to get my mouthpiece, and there was another kid in there, an older kid. I startled him. He pulls a gun out and says, "Tell anyone about this, and I'll kill you." Me, "OK!" I sprinted out of there. I did not tell a soul. Not my cousins, who were counselors at the camp. Not even my parents when they picked me up. Nope. I kept that to myself for years. To me, at 12 years old, fear was real.

The coach blew the whistle. Mike and I jumped up; I ran toward him, and he at me. I was scared out of my mind. Mike just looked tough. Me, I did not look tough at all. I was spindly. Mike's eyes bulged as he sprinted right for me. My eyes slammed shut as I tip-toed in his direction like a deer. Told you I was scared. BAM! I thought I had died right there. Mike hit me so hard. He put his shoulder right in my stomach. There I was, on my back, writhing in pain, the whole team looking at me. Who knows where the ball went? I did not care. I was crying and could not breathe. Meanwhile, our coach kneels over me. "Calm down, Billy. You are ok. He got you good. Just settle down and breathe." In my head, I am like, good? That was good? Breathe?

Me: I can't breathe, Coach.

Coach: You got the wind knocked out of you, Billy. You will be ok. Just relax.

Coach reached down and pulled my pants up away from my waist. That helped a lot! I finally got up and went to the back of the line. No one said a word to me. I counted the players in each line to make sure I did not have to go against Mike again. If so, I was either jumping in front of someone or letting the teammate behind me go ahead of me. I was not going through that again!

Mike and I became good friends. Our moms would drop each of us off at the other one's house to hang out. I would mention the fact that he tried to kill me in practice. We both laughed. Mike was a beast in 95-lb football. Countless times, we would see him racing up and down the football field, eluding tacklers and scoring touchdowns. He was amazing! Everyone knew he would be great. Years later, Mike attended a university where he played free safety and crushed it, no doubt.

It turns out, I was surprisingly good once I got the hang of 95-lb football. I played quarterback. Other than fumbling on the first play when my "girlfriend" came to see me play, I was exciting to watch. Especially if you were my mom. I have vivid memories of her watching me on the sidelines. Running down the sideline with me, literally, almost stride for stride, yelling, "Go, Billy! Go! That's my baby!" No joke.

The fun stopped when my mom, dad and I went to Danny's Spaghetti House in Silver Spring for dinner. My mom, exasperated, was upset, and said to my dad, "Every time Billy gets the team down to the endzone, they put the other boy in the game. The coach is prejudiced. I'm tired of this!" They were talking about taking me off the team. I was not having it. I started crying and carrying on, so much so that a lady at the next table interrupted the conversation. She thought my parents were abusing me. Once she heard the whole story, then she just piled on. "Ohhhhhhh, yeahhhh. No, that is not right. You get the team all the way down the field; then they put the little white boy in the game to get the glory? Ah hell naw. That ain't right."

I do not remember if I finished out the season. I do not remember not finishing out the season. Whether my coach was prejudiced or not, being taken out of the game every time I drove us down the field, then being replaced by my teammate and watching him reap the benefits, affected me. Regardless of what I was "told" by my parents, my mind programmed, "you can't finish." Why? Because the opportunity to finish, to experience the elation of completing the drive with a touchdown, was taken away from me.

If you prepare to run a 100-meter race by running eighty meters each practice, you will come up short every time! If you practice running for a 100-meter race by running one hundred meters every practice, but then you are stopped short of the white tape, then you will never reach the finish line. It is hard to learn what you are not taught. It is even harder to unlearn what has been programmed.

As a boy, quite often, I bit off more than I cared to chew. I was so excited to play the violin, but after three lessons, I wanted to quit. My parents made me tough it out for a year. The same went for the saxophone. One year. The drums were different, though! My parents emphatically said, "NO!" Even though my mom and dad drilled into me the importance of "finishing what you start," I still wrestled with getting things done. In retrospect, did my parents' threats to remove me from the football team affect me? Did the thought of being removed add to the anxiety? Yes, to both, probably. But that had nothing to do with me struggling to finish what I started. Plain and simple, I lacked discipline. Over time, I queried why I still struggled with completing certain projects in my later years. Much of it had to do with me trying to do too much and less to do with discipline.

As with all service academies, discipline is of the utmost importance at the Naval Academy. They drilled it into me and my classmates at NAPS. It was also drilled into us during my four years in Annapolis, especially Plebe Summer. You already know it is chaotic. Therefore, be assertive, be efficient, be in uniform, be there for your classmates, and DON'T BE LATE. There is something to be said about being on time for formation, in the right uniform, and inspection ready. They do not just expect it from you. They demand it. Conversely, if for ANY REASON one is late, out of uniform, not ready for inspection, or all of the above, THERE IS HELL TO PAY. Enter Pape Meissa Khoule. He was my roommate during the plebe summer. Meissa was from Senegal, Africa. He validated classes while in-flight to Annapolis. This brother was brilliant. As intelligent as he was, to me, at least, at that moment, he lacked common sense. Do not misunderstand me. I love Meissa like a brother. We experienced mountains of misery together. But what he did this one day gave me pause.

It was a normal, hectic, crazy, head-spinning plebe summer day. We had 5 minutes to undress, shower, dress, be inspection-ready, and in formation. FIVE MINUTES! That means our shower is seconds long, not minutes. I jump out of the shower, I start getting into uniform, and Khoule is still in PT gear (shorts and t-shirt), barefooted, with his legs propped up on his desk, reading the paper. I am flying around, all the while checking my rack, locker, and items for gear adrift. I yelled at him,

Me: KHOULE! WHAT THE HECK! WHAT ARE YOU DOING? WE GOT 2 MINUTES TIL FORMATION!

Meissa: **Khoule is taking a break. He is tired. Khoule will relax and read the newspaper."**

Me: KHOULE WILL WHAT? WHY ARE YOU TALKING TO ME IN THE THIRD PERSON? BRO, ARE YOU CRAZY? NEWSPAPER? WE GOT 1 MINUTE NOW! Khoule, I cannot go out there without my roommate. You know the rules. Come on, man! I cannot stay here either. Then I will be late for formation! They will kill me man. They already do not like me because I am a football player! LET'S GO!

Me: Khoule will rest now.

I sprinted down the hallway to formation. I made it on time. Our platoon commander, Mr. Smith, was no joke. I do not think he liked himself. So, I know he did not like anybody else, especially us plebes. He was plain mean! He was waiting on the headcount from the squad leaders.

Squad Leader: We're missing one, sir.

Mr. Smith: WHAT!? WHO!? WHO'S MISSING!?

Squad Leader: Looks like, Khoule, sir. I don't see him.

Mr. Smith: YANCEY, WHERE'S MR. KHOULE!? HE'S YOUR ROOMMATE!?

I did not say a word. I was freaking out inside. Smith came running over and jumped in my face.

Mr. Smith: YANCEY, ARE YA DEAF? WHERE'S KHOULE?!

Me: No, excuse sir!

We had five basic responses, and 'I don't know, sir' or 'He's tired and reading the newspaper, sir" are not any of them! My choices were Yes Sir, No Sir, Aye-Aye Sir, I'll Find Out Sir, and No Excuse Sir. Considering the circumstances, No Excuse, Sir, was my best and safest response.

Mr. Smith: WHAT! NO EXCUSE?! YOU'RE DAMN RIGHT, MR. YANCEY! THERE'S NO EXCUSE FOR YOU! NOW WHERE'S MR. KOOL!

Smith stormed away, headed down the corridor to me and Khoule's room. Our squad leader was right behind him.

Mr. Smith: KHOULE, WHERE THE HELL ARE YOU?! YOU BETTER BE PASSED OUT OR DEAD! YOU BETTER NOT MAKE US LATE FOR CHOW!

They finally reached our room. We could hear the door crash open.

Mr. Smith: WHAT THE HELL ARE YOU DOING, MR. KOOL!? READING THE NEWSPAPER? YOU'RE TIRED? WELL, LOOKIE HERE! GET UP MR. KOOL! YOU CAN READ

THE NEWSPAPER ON YOUR OWN TIME! RIGHT NOW, YOU'RE ON MY TIME! YOU'RE ON THE NAVY'S TIME! NOW GET UP!

We heard the chair slide across the floor and then scurrying. Our squad leader raced back, then led us down to eat lunch. Khoule and Mr. Smith were eating alongside us shortly thereafter. Khoule had a different attitude. Let me tell you. He never did that again. And if anybody else was thinking about it, NOPE. It did not happen.

I recall something similar happening at the end of my junior year. As a rising senior, I spent a week with each service community to help me decide on my career path. So, one week with the Marine Corps, one week with Navy aviation, one week on a submarine, and one week on a surface ship. I was in Quantico, Virginia, with the Marines. There was a group of Naval Academy rising sophomores there the same week as me. One of them had a real problem with being on time, and he was always joking around. It just so happened that this same kid was late again. This time, instead of his company officer disciplining him, the Gunnery Sergeant stepped forward and said, "I got this one, sir. No problem." He motioned to the youngster, "Come with me."

At the time, instructions about the O-Course had everyone's attention. I forgot all about Gunny and the kid. Anyway, when they returned about an hour later, it was a brand-new kid. I do not know what Gunny did or said, but it worked. Not a peep out of this kid for the rest of his time in Quantico. Nothing! I asked Gunny,

Me: Gunny, what did you do to that boy?

Gunny: Aw, sir, we just had a conversation. It's what we Gunnies do.

Me: Roger that, Gunny.

And that is all I needed to know. We had a Gunnery Sergeant Osbourne at NAPS who was strikingly similar. I understood implicitly. So, what is the lesson? DISCIPLINE! BE DISCIPLINED! Do what they tell you to do. Do not try to buck the system, even if you are tired and want to read the newspaper or be the class clown. Be a team player, and finish what you set out to do. If you are in a game and your coach sends in a substitution for you, should you get an attitude and come out or be obstinate and stay in? No. Lose the attitude and come out of the game. ONE, it is bigger than you. TWO, coach rules. THREE, refer to RULE NUMBER TWO. No matter how talented you are or what you and your personal fan club may think, you are not bigger than the team and certainly not bigger than the game. So, leave all of that "Me Me Me" on the bus. Team first. I am encouraging you to be the best version of yourself spiritually, physically, mentally, athletically, and professionally. Do not give anyone a reason to take you off the field, off the court, off the committee, or down from the podium. Reach for the top always. Coach was not overwhelmingly confident with the outcome when I got close to the finish line, or rather, with me taking the team into the end zone. In the end, do not give anyone a reason to remove you. The value of participating with you should exceed the value of participating without you. Do your best, maintain discipline, and let the chips fall where they may. Whether you are the chosen one or not, discipline wins in the end. I implore you to inculcate this in your brain. This is a game-changer. I do not know what became of the midshipman straightened out by Gunny. I do know that my classmate, Meissa Khoule, is the Deputy President General of the newly created Defense of Senegal for the Joint War and Staff Colleges. Not sure if

the newspaper incident was the catalyst. I do not recommend you try
it.

Chapter Three: Never Settle!

"Blessed is the one who perseveres under trial because, having stood the test, that person will receive the crown of life that the Lord has promised to those who love him."
James 1:12 NIV

Water seeks its own level, and so do people. Not only can we be products of our environment, but we can also be products sold for cheap and not even know it. As often as we have heard, read, or said, "Be yourself" or "to thine own self be true," have you kept your promise? I mean, really. Have you? Have you worked to be your best you, or have you worked to be someone else's version of you?

Denzel Washington says, "Just because you're doing a lot more, doesn't mean you're getting a lot more done!" This was me 100%. I was out of the Navy with my personal training business underway. My Billy Bodies business cards and T-shirts were sweet. I thought I was hot stuff. I had an OK client base, a few in-home clients, but the rest came to Flex Gym, where I was an independent contractor. In my head, I was doing great because I was training a handful of clients. I thought I was putting in work.

It was not enough. I could never catch the money up with my bills, or vice versa. This was problematic. I had spending issues. I went through money like it was water. I also had a fear of money, and at the same time, I could never make enough of it. To make matters worse, someone told me that if I did not make a certain amount of money per year, then I did not have to pay taxes. I have also learned that if we look hard enough and ask enough people, we can find whatever answer for which we are searching. So, for a while, I made money, drove around in my BMW, lived with a roommate, bought stuff, juggled bills, paid the "minimum" on my credit cards, and shunned taxes. Money was my conundrum. The harder I worked to make money, the more I spent. The more I spent on frivolous things, the deeper the hole I dug. Poor management? Not even close. This was much worse. Bedlam.

Finally, the solution. I found it. One of my clients owned a horse farm. He was short-handed and needed help. He asked if I was interested, and I obliged, of course. I asked what I would be doing, and he said cleaning stalls. I had no idea what this entailed, but I needed the money badly.

As a kid, I cleaned my room, the kitchen, the basement, the backyard, etc. You know? Responsibilities. Chores. In college, I cleaned up my room, helped clean our company area, cleaned outside when I got in trouble and was on restriction, cleaned my car, etc. You know? Responsibilities. Chores.

Chris, the owner, showed me how to clean a stall. It seemed pretty straightforward, but. Couple things. One, this was the furthest from any chore I ever encountered. The experience was like no other, especially since a horse was usually in the stall with me while I cleaned it. And, if you cannot make the *short clicking noise* with your mouth to make the horse move, then you can forget it. I would just move to the next stall. I was not arguing with a horse. There were over 30 stalls. He was bound to move eventually.

Two, the *wet spot,* which was usually inconveniently resting back in a corner underneath the 2000-lb. horse, took a fair amount of work to scrape, dig out, and cover back up with fresh hay.

Three, it was not so much the cleaning of the stall that was laborious. Standing in a 12 x 12 box next to a horse weighing a ton that could crush me at any moment, I was one scared city boy.

But there was much more for this city boy to fear than a 2000-lb horse once his 120-lb mother discovered he was moonlighting at a farm. As you already know, my mother did not play. She was known as Reverend Dr. Jean Robinson Casey. I called her Ma. Both gave me a tongue-lashing that I will never forget. On a Monday afternoon, when most 9-5ers are getting off work, which is also the busiest time for most gyms, I was sitting in one of the owners' chairs between the front door and counter. It was a black and red director's chair. This was no ordinary chair. It was Big Al's chair. He was one of the owners. Big Al was legendary. He was a mentor to all of us. I will share more about him later.

In any event, I was sitting in Big Al's chair, thinking I was cool because I was seated in Big Al's chair. I was relaxing, chatting it up with members on their way in and out of the gym. Ma walks in. I lean forward to get up, and in a low, calm voice, she says, "Don't get up." To myself, I said, "This isn't good." I got my very own personal sermon right in front of everybody coming and going. A few stayed just to watch. Here is the thing. The only person that could hear what she was saying was me. Yes, she was that close to me, and her voice was low. It was low, but I could hear her roar. That was good and bad. In fact, it made it worse. I could hear every single word, vowel, consonant, tone, and pitch. She articulated each word deeply, succinctly, and intentionally. I heard and felt each word deeply, succinctly, and intentionally. Part of me wanted one of those 2000-lb. horses standing in front of me instead of Ma. But I digress.

A few times I attempted to get a word in, and she would calmly and slowly raise her hand and let out a quick "uh." Back to receive mode I went and stayed. This went on for about 10 minutes. That is a long time to get lectured, especially in front of your friends, members, clients, Big Al and staff. My mom's eyes never left mine, and if I looked away, then a swift "uh" was deployed. Here is an excerpt:

"Listen here, son. I didn't work two jobs, sometimes three, scraping to put food on the table, clothes on your back, and pay tuition to Landon, send you off to the Naval Academy and graduate, and then become an officer in the United States Navy, to have you shoveling horse manure!"

Now, stretch that over 10 minutes and what you have is good old unadulterated humiliation. That was by far one of my most embarrassing moments in life. I was disappointed after it was over, but I appreciate it, nonetheless. I had gone awry. Hey, there is nothing wrong with cleaning stalls. It is not the career path I was educated to pursue. Some may say, "Well, there's nothing wrong with a second job. There is nothing wrong with manual labor." I agree. Both are formidable practices. But personally, I am highly capable in other ways. I was just not applying myself. My mom's wake-up call, in the presence of all my friends and workmates, was justified. I needed it. I embraced it. I hung up my shovel immediately.

This was one of many lessons that I learned from the amazing woman that birthed me. My mom began her professional career as an educator. All the challenges and throes that it took for her to obtain her degree was A LOT. Along with my grandmother taking care of me for a few weeks at her home in Richmond, VA, while my mom traveled to Washington DC to find a daycare facility for me, to rising in the wee hours every day readying me for pick up at 5:30 am by Dr. Yancey, director of Tiny Tot Day Care, to attending DC Teachers College all day, to a part-time job following classes, then finally picking me up from daycare at 5 pm, my mom was spent. This began when I was 2 years old and lasted for a few years. We lived in my mother's sister's, Aunt Jewell's, basement. I have vivid memories of giant clowns painted on two of the closet doors. They kept me up at night. They were always watching me.

In retrospect, the path that my mother took to teach children at Lafayette Elementary School was par for the course. She later continued higher education to accomplish her Master of Divinity degree and then her Doctor of Ministry degree. And now, along with my stepfather, Reverend Clyde, pastor's Martin Luther King Jr Christian Church in Reston, Virginia. I am inspired by my mother's pursuit and achievement to lead, preach, and teach others to live healthier, stronger lives. I am attempting to follow in her footsteps.

Due to friends, family, foes, or our own negligence, we occasionally settle and do not even realize it. We start off with our own rules and standards to live by, intermix with the world, and suddenly, without warning, we are living with a different mindset and completely different values. I meant what I said earlier about going from person to person in search of a *certain answer*. That is real. If someone believes it is okay to wear their pants inside out with the pockets and zipper showing, then all it will take is for one person to agree. Suddenly, it is a thing that morphs into a habit. What is next? People walk around with their pants inside out, thinking it is cool, and it is not.

Or better yet, a person who has poor spending habits has a conversation with someone who does not understand the tax code. This is problematic. I lived it. It is easy to slip into a lower gear and cruise along, thinking you are going in the right direction, when truthfully, you are driving against traffic. An accident is imminent. Every now and then, I encourage frequent recalibration. Check yourself. If not you, then have a friend or family member hold you accountable. It works if you work it. Never settle!

Chapter Four: Faith!

"For nothing will be impossible with God."
ESV

Of all the battles in my life, my son William's was the toughest! William was born 14 weeks early on September 11, 2006, at 1:32 am. Full-term birth is 40 weeks. He only weighed 1-lb.-14ozs. He fit in the palm of my hand. William had a serious brain bleed in both hemispheres. The brain matter in the left hemisphere was gone.

William has cerebral palsy. It is a disorder that affects the muscles and never goes away. It affects movement. One of the side effects is spasticity; his arm and leg muscles are constantly contracted. All caused by an undeveloped brain, related to his early birth.

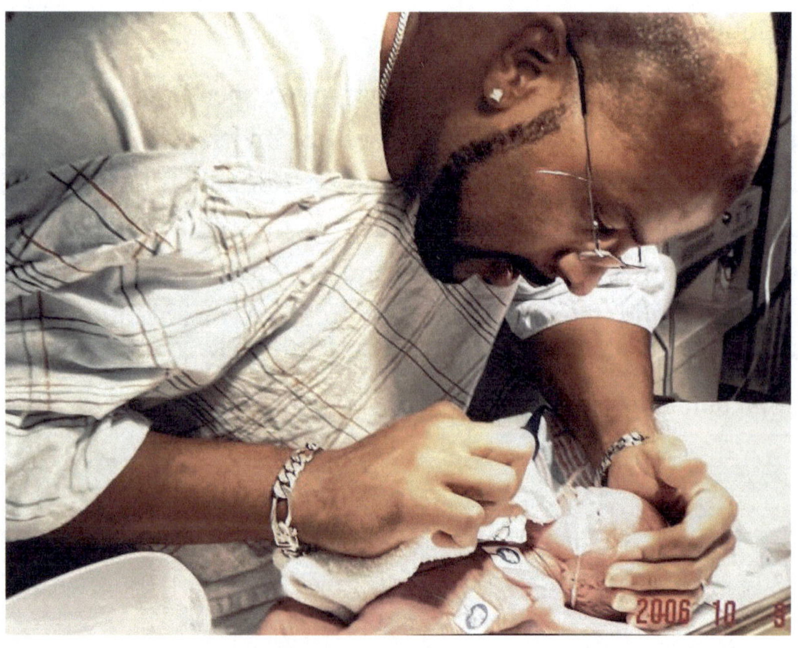

I recall our family meeting with his doctor. The information he shared was very cold, dark, and devastating. He did not give William a chance. Dr. Doubt said if we kept William, then he would be blind, deaf, eat and drink from a straw, and be stuck in a wheelchair with no quality of life. He finished by saying that 65% of these cases FAIL. Dead silence filled the room. His words cut each of us to the core. My father, Clyde, vehemently affirmed, "We believe in a Higher Being. We will go with the 35%." "If William is in there fighting, then we're out here fighting and praying for him," I added.

I drafted this poem that describes how I felt alongside William in the NICU:

When I was a little boy, one of my favorite things to do was play my Mattel Handheld Football Game. It was a little bigger than an iPhone. It was about 6" long and 3.5" wide. William was barely twice that size when he was born. It was all white and had six small buttons to play defense, kick, and score touchdowns. The object of the game was to defend and score. I loved it. I would play it for hours and lost all sense of time. When you scored, a cluster of beeps would play. I will never forget the melody.

As I sat at William's bedside in the NICU, I would often hear a cluster of beeps. Our little boy was hooked up to a myriad of machines. Like my Mattel Handheld, but not just one. Many! Similar but much different. This was no game. The beeps were indicators, not touchdowns. The indicators of oxygen flowing came from a pulse oximeter machine that helped measure the oxygen level in his blood. But there was the other monitor that tracked William's heart rate and breaths per minute, known as an apnea/Brady monitor(A/B). Normal limits for oxygen saturation were 93% or above, an absolute must to keep William's tiny body and organs receiving enough oxygenation through blood flow. The A/B monitor measured William's breaths and heart rate every minute. Normal breaths for preemies like William back then were 30-53 per minute and a heart rate between 100-205 beats per minute. Indicators of breathing. Indicators of life. The beeps were constant in the beginning. Intimidating. Overpowering. Annoying! They seemed to play for hours. I would lose all sense of time. After a while, it was just background noise. All was well until that dreaded squeal! A high-pitched sound followed by a really low, dull growl. I will never forget the melody.

I loathed that sound! It meant that William was experiencing a wave of problems: not enough breaths per minute, apnea where he stopped breathing for 20 seconds or more, had a low or high heart rate, or he was not getting enough oxygenation throughout his body. Many times, the alarms screamed due to several indicators that lots were going awry in our baby boy. When William lost his breath, I held mine. When his heart slowed, my heart raced and sank. The six small buttons to defend and score were nowhere in sight. I felt helpless.

There is scared, and there is afraid. I was afraid! Look at William, look at the monitor, look up for a nurse. Look at William, look at the monitor, look up for a nurse. LOOK AT WILLIAM! LOOK AT THE MONITOR! LOOK UP FOR A NURSE! Finally, a nurse! She gets William settled, resets the monitor, "He's fine," she says and walks away. "Phew." I would exhale. Like when I was a little boy when I thought I lost my Mattel Handheld. Look in my room, look under my bed, look under the couch. Look in my room, look under my bed, look under the couch. My mom! She would find it, settle me down, hand it to me, and walk away. "Phew." I would exhale. Similar but much different...

I will never forget Dr. Doubt telling us that the wise decision would be to let William go. That was never an option. There is a teaching about the finger and the moon. "The teaching is merely a vehicle to describe truth. Do not mistake it for the truth itself. A finger pointing at the moon is not the moon. The finger is needed to know where to look for the moon, but if you mistake the finger for the moon itself, you will never know."

On September 10, 2006, the evening before William was born, despite the discomfort and cramping William's mom was experiencing, the nurses on call, after administering a lengthy ultrasound, assured us, "Everything is OK." As a father, husband, and human being, I had absolutely no reason to think otherwise. My expectations as we drove away from the hospital and headed home were that everything was OK. Well, everything was not OK. Just hours later, our world went sideways!

Here I was, racing back to the hospital. What was going on? I never asked God why. William was born 14 weeks early, under 2-lbs, with multiple complications, yet I never asked God, "Why, my son?" Nope, not once.

I was going through hell, it seemed. Thinking back, I did not want anyone to ask me, "Are you OK?" NO. But, of course, I would lie. I was not OK! I was in pain. Sometimes I would hear, "I know how you feel." NO, YOU DON'T. Let me tell you something. When you are in your own skin, no one feels it like you do. I was in a constant mental and emotional battle. At times, it was as if I were in a trance.

That was my way of dealing with the pain. Ignore. Ignore. Ignore. In my mind, those babies were Goliath. William was David! It was not long before I, myself, started calling William, Jumbo. His mother,

Lisa, hated that. Looking back, it was my way of seeing my son as bigger than life. He was tiny. But he was my world.

In spite of William's tumultuous entry into the world, my grandmother, William's great-grandmother, the late Doris Robinson Griffin, seemed to be as one with the Holy Spirit. She would be known as a pastor in today's climate. Back in her era, the 1950's, women were not recognized as such. Nevertheless, she was a renowned guest speaker all over the country for various Christian denominations, as well as a mentor to hundreds of men, women, and children. William's great-grandmother helped raise 4 amazing kids who are my mother, aunt, and 2 uncles. She was Valedictorian of her high school class, a devoted Baptist church member, chairperson of the board of Christian education, and Virginia's President of Church Women's United.

While holding William in the NICU shortly after he was born, she gazed at him and declared, "This child will live." She snuggled William up to her as if her own baby boy. There she sat for hours, holding him, rocking him, and praying for him. Grandma Griffin prayed incessantly, and the Almighty answered her prayers in droves.

Although Doris passed on when William was but the age of five, the blessings she passed onto him were immense: love, strength, fight, will, joy, energy, focus, determination, and serenity. It was fascinating to watch them together. She loved William. And William loved her right back.

The apple does not fall too far from the tree. If that is the case, and William is the apple and Lisa and I are the tree, then how strong are we? How strong am I? I just did not see it that way. At times, I felt weak. I felt powerless. I felt like there was nothing I could do for my son. That made my heart hurt. I still marvel at William's strength. He went through it all. A turbulent birth that was fourteen weeks early, 92 days in the Children's Hospital Neonatal Intensive Care Unit, over the years amassed eighteen eye surgeries, five brain surgeries, four spinal taps, three dental surgeries, two hernia surgeries, one central line surgery, twenty-nine total, and William continues to thrive daily.

Yet, I never asked God why, until I visited a friend and his wife in the hospital about two years after William was born. It was days before William's second birthday. They had a little boy. I held him for a while. I will never forget how blown away I was. I was holding a newborn in a hospital, in a private room with a TV, carry-out pizza, with no monitors, no oxygen, no beeps, no Bradycardia and no apnea. I WAS HOLDING A BABY, AND I WASN'T IN A NICU. Frankly, it was very strange. I did not say anything to my friends. I just sat there numb. Their baby boy was gazing at me, and I was gazing right back, in awe. I said my goodbyes, held their bundle of joy one more time and left.

As I walked out of the room, I began to cry. I held on until I got back to my car. I had all the happiness in the world for my friends and their newborns. So happy that they gave birth to a perfectly healthy baby boy. On the other hand, I was in anguish. I lost it completely when I shut my door. Meltdown. I had never held a baby in a hospital outside of a NICU. Why couldn't we have been in a normal room with our son? Why was William so different? God, what have I done wrong? God, why my son? God, why? Why? Why? Why? Why? Why? I drove away. I needed windshield wipers, and it was not raining.

I never asked why because I did not think I had a right to question God. I was me, and God was God. That was that. Finally, I could not take it anymore. I questioned God. I deserved to know why. If God were going to punish me for questioning Him, then, in my mind's eye, He couldn't hurt me anymore than I was already hurting, so I thought. I had hit the bottom. I had nothing left.

Today, William is 17 years old. He is in high school, loves to attend classes with his schoolmates, walks with a crutch on his own, has great vision and impeccable hearing, enjoys hitting, throwing, and running the bases on his baseball team, as well as draining 3-point shots on the basketball court. William is extremely bright. Nothing short of amazing. His favorite subjects are math and PE and he even enjoys singing in the chorus. One of his favorite songs he loves to sing is "Hallelujah." How about that! His late great-grandmother, Doris, would be so proud. We are, too. In middle school, William was the manager of the basketball team. They even gave him a uniform. He was #4! This is so special because William's favorite sport, hobby, and leisure pursuit is basketball.

In fact, God blessed William with the opportunity to meet his idol, his hero, his favorite athlete, five-time all-star guard, Steph Curry. We traveled to Washington, DC, to see him and the Golden State Warriors play the Washington Wizards. It was exciting and, at the same time, nerve-racking, because we were not 100% sure that William would be able to meet his G.O.A.T…

There, we waited, erratically patiently, outside the arena with countless other fans anxious to get inside. Finally, an usher scurried William, his mom, and me through a checkpoint, onto an elevator, downstairs and outside the Warriors locker room. YOU TALK ABOUT NERVOUS. WOW! There, we waited for Steph to come out. The referee walked into the locker room to get him but came back out by himself. He told us that he was not sure if we would be able to meet Steph because he was already on the court warming up. My stomach was in KNOTS.

Anyway, off to the court we went. There we were at the edge of the basketball court by the Warriors' bench, our eyes bulging out, watching Steph warm up. I cannot put into words the anticipation we all felt at that moment. The emotions are indescribable. We wanted nothing more than for our son to have his moment. FINALLY! IT HAPPENED! Steph waltzed over, started up a conversation with William, handed him a basketball; William dribbled, and passed it back to Steph. SPLASH! History! William threw him an assist for a 3-point jump shot. It was magical! William got his autograph and then shared an unforgettable fist bump.

What was most interesting, was William's demeanor during the 3 minutes spent with Steph. I thought he would have gone berserk. Not even close. Totally at peace. Despite his calm, cool, collectiveness, that moment WENT VIRAL. Although the meeting lasted minutes, this supernatural moment was broadcasted on the **Today Show, ESPN, Inside the NBA,** the **Golden State Warriors** webpage, and the cover of the **Washington Post Sports** page. By far, one of the most amazing experiences of my life. Overjoyed for William!

The blessings keep rolling in. William continues to excel in school, therapy, and everyday life. He is on the Principal's Advisory Group of his middle school; he is walking independently with one crutch, stepping over barriers, as well as stepping side to side and being involved more at home, helping to load and unload the dishwasher, take the trash out, and put his dishes in the sink after eating. William is doing things daily that doctors never foresaw. He continues to push the envelope in ways that most thought impossible. William is unstoppable. His best is yet to come.

A close friend, Sharon, said to me one day, "Not all of God's gifts come wrapped in a pretty red bow." Over the years, I have grown to have a greater appreciation for her kind words. Sharon was 100 percent right! Life has an uncanny way of revealing our greatest blessings.

The lesson is to **HAVE FAITH**! Even when things look bleak, I encourage you to believe in a positive outcome. Faith is believing when common sense says not to. William was born abnormally early. He was a micro preemie. He fit in the palm of my hand. My wedding ring, fit like a hula hoop around his leg. He had serious brain bleeds in both hemispheres. The brain matter in the left hemisphere was gone. He was in the NICU for 92 days. The doctor predicted no vision, no hearing, meals through a straw, and an inferior quality of life engulfed by a wheelchair. William's fight looked insurmountable. But God! William's determination to fight produced a miracle.

I believe everything that happens to us happens for us. Individually and collectively, we all are on paths specified for our lifetime. Our trails will cross others until our time is up. How others' lives play out is not up to us. Why some have and others have not, is not our concern, nor is it our place to judge. "Stay in your lane" are words I live by. Embrace His grace. Keep the faith!

Chapter Five: Failure!

"My flesh and my heart may fail, but God is the strength of my heart and my portion forever."
Psalm 73:26 NIV

Mike Tyson said, "Everyone has a plan until they get punched in the mouth." Life punched me in the mouth! I failed to plan! I sucker-punched myself over and over again! If I received a dollar for every time I failed along these 55 years, I would be a richer man. Because of my iniquities, I am rich with wisdom and seeking more every day. I failed so many times that I had to give my pep talk a pep talk. Thank God I never gave up. Bowing out of a relationship is giving up or quitting in conversations of today's world. I disagree. If it does not work, then it does not work. Far be it from me to try and make my significant other think more like me or vice versa. Move on. I have never had a problem with pulling chocks, making way to get underway. It has been my experience that my failures have been tremendous teaching tools.

My mother used to tell me that when it came to girlfriends, I had a *two-year rule*. As in my relationships, they never went past two years. She was right! In retrospect, as I ponder, countless failed relationships ventured beyond the expiration date, two years, and eventually fell apart. Imagine that. I was doing something wrong. I should have listened to my mother.

Subsequently, I have had two divorces. In both cases, I could have put forth more effort. A common thread was that I was not "present." I am an entrepreneur. I own a fitness technology company. I am a workaholic. My day starts at 4 a.m.; then, I typically do not get home until around 7 p.m. at the earliest. As soon as I get home, I change clothes and immediately gather my clothes and meals for the next day. Every day, like clockwork. In another relationship, my girlfriend called me a robot. She was sarcastically serious, but I was always ready to roll when I woke up the next morning. Truthfully, my robotic behaviors were not conducive to building a strong family or strong relationship with my partner. I understand that now. I could have been a better husband. I could have been a better partner. I could have been, should have been, and was not. You know, admitting that I have no regrets is selfish, but that is where I was at the time. I was not a good fit.

But, in my first marriage, being Roger Robot was not my only flaw. I was not a good person all around. I had some unpleasant habits and traits. I was unfaithful. I drank heavily. I experimented with drugs. I was selfish. I was all about me. I asked the Sprint associate to change the last four digits of my phone number to spell SWOL as in swollen, big, huge. I was majorly arrogant. In my head, I believed I would change when we got married. Not even close. Events do not change your bad habits. Practicing good habits makes good habits. Practicing good habits solidifies better habits. I was so used to practicing bad habits that I thought my bad habits were good. Well, they were good for me, at least. There it is again. All about me.

I was in a dark space. I recall one friend telling me, "Get as many women as you can and want. Don't you know what they said in the Old Testament? That is the way they used to do it. Go for it." I did not know anything about the Old Testament or the New Testament, much less anything else in the Bible. I was Bible illiterate. Another friend told me to date married women because they have something to lose. They will think twice about giving you a tough time because they have a husband and family at home and will not want to take the risk. Hey, what are friends for, right? Remember earlier when I said, if we look hard enough and ask enough people, we can find whatever answer for which we are searching? Well, here I was again. I did not care to be faithful. My friends gave me more of a reason to keep doing wrong. My friends validated my behaviors. I was like the men in the Bible. Boy, how holy was I? I was a real Christian. I was a complete JACKASS.

How many mistakes would I have to make until I finally straightened up? COUNTLESS. The only way to start climbing out of a hole is to stop digging. Trying to make progress by climbing upward and digging downward at the same time is IMPOSSIBLE. I stopped seeing "so and so" outside of my marriage *as much*, and I thought this was my saving grace. NO. That is like saying we are kinda pregnant. Huh? You cannot *kinda* cheat. You cannot kinda drink or kinda do drugs either. Either you DO or you DON'T. I did them all. The problem is, when you do dirt, you get dirty.

Fortunately, over time, I would stop all of my wayward behaviors. Not all at once, but I eventually eliminated them all. Cheating in my relationships was no longer an option. I nixed drinking alcohol because when I drank, I broke out in jackass. And I stopped using drugs because I did not get out of them what I thought I would. I believed that I would feel better, look better, and be more accomplished by using performance-enhancing and recreational drugs. I was wrong. High blood pressure, high cholesterol, heart palpitations, and horrendous blood work were normal for me. Every time I went to my doctor for a checkup, after taking my blood pressure, the nurse would tell me, "You better be careful, Mr. Yancey. You are going to mess around and stroke out if you don't start taking better care of yourself." She would walk out; then I would dismiss everything she said to me.

During my bodybuilding years, low body fat, muscle size and tightness was the ultimate goal on stage. One of the mantras that I learned was, "The closer you get to death, the better you look." Meaning, the tighter, more vascular, and dehydrated you are, the better you look on stage. So, clearly, my goal was to look as close to dead as possible.

A conversation with an old gym friend was eye-opening. He was in medical school at the time. His words changed my life forever. He said, "It's all good and well on the outside. If you could see what is going on in your insides, then you would know why drugs are not good for you. They are killing your insides, Billy." He further questioned the authenticity of the substances I was taking. "It's probably fake or dangerous for your body. That is why we have doctors like endocrinologists who can tell us, if needed, how much of a prescribed drug or supplement we should take. This one-size-fits-all approach, where you guess how much you should take, is dangerous." Back then, "more is better" was contagious. One of the bodybuilders I idolized claimed, "a syringe not filled to the top was a wasted syringe." So, what did I do? I filled it up! That talk with my friend was the closer for me. That was it. That was all I needed to hear. Done deal. I encourage the same for you. Do not do it. IT IS NOT WORTH IT. The truth is anything can happen. A drug or drugs may affect you differently than someone else. Just because Billy Meathead is taking a drug that is not giving him "adverse side effects," SO HE SAYS, does not mean that it cannot happen to you. Case in point, after giving myself numerous injections in my butt, it got to the point where it was extremely painful to continue getting a shot in that area. I heard some guys were taking in their chests, and it was just as effective. I asked another friend of mine what he thought, and he said,

Friend: Whoa! In your chest, bro! Dang! I don't know about that. That sounds kinda dicey to me. Just take it in your thigh.

Me: That hurts like hell! Nah. I'll just take it in my chest. I'll be good!

Friend: Good luck!!!

Well, that was a mistake. My left pec swelled up like a pumpkin. I was freaking out! Here I was, in the middle of the summer, wearing long-sleeved shirts to hide my chest. I went to my doctor. She said, "You obviously hit something that made your chest angry." She had never seen this before. Imagine that. She just told me to give it about a week. That the swelling should decrease by itself.

Me: A WEEK!?

Doctor: Yes, Mr. Yancey. I bet you won't do that again.

I just walked out. I was so frustrated. I was walking around with what looked like a woman's breast! Finally, about a week later, the swelling went down. NEVER AGAIN. But here is the thing. More often than not, one of the popular statements is, "That could never happen to me." Well, you would be wrong. It happened to me. If it can happen to me, then it can most certainly happen to you, too.

Listen, folks. I was corrupt. I even knew of a pastor who had some corrupt behaviors as well, so again, relationship-wise, I figured my actions were justified. But that is no excuse either. THERE IS NO EXCUSE FOR ANY OF MY SINFUL BEHAVIORS OR

INIQUITIES. Here is the thing. When you partake in wrong, then more wrong persists and multiplies. Playing a small part in a large infraction is still an infraction. Part of the sickness was thinking that I was getting away with it. The plausibility of invisibility is a mirage. Even when I believed that no one saw me or thought no one saw me, I was seen every time. *I was never not seen. He is watching always.* Take heed or pay the piper. I paid dearly for years.

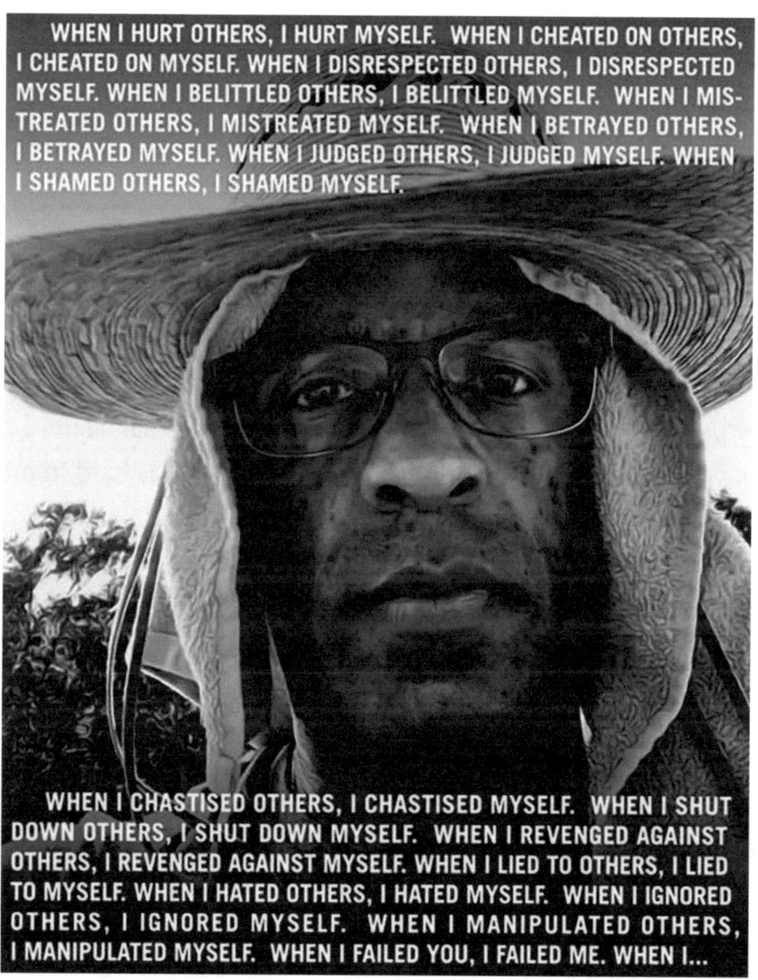

During my first marriage, I cheated on my wife. Yes, I committed adultery with a woman I had known for a long time. She even came to my barbershop. I was at her house earlier, then later walked into the barbershop to get a haircut, reached to take off my glasses, and they were not on my face. I leaned back in the chair with my hands covering my face. Oh no! I texted her, and minutes later, she walked into the barbershop, handed me my glasses, and then walked out. Of course, right then, all eyes were on me. I played it up like I was a Mac daddy. I was nothing more than a foolish man cheating on his wife. We were both cheaters, and few knew about us until that day. Not even my wife. We dated off and on for years. Did we get away with it? No way. Not a chance. He knew. God knew.

What is even crazier is that years later, long after being divorced from my first and second wives, I thought a relationship could survive with this woman. I believed that because I was single when I started dating this same woman, who originally was part of my infidelity many years prior, that I was starting anew with a clean slate. I could not have been more wrong. Now, thinking back to it is hard to process for me. Today, I would not even consider going outside of my relationship. I was living a lie. When living a lie, you compromise yourself and others around you, because lying has a ripple effect. Hence, many of my relationships were inorganic. There lay my problems. Fruit of a tainted tree.

After 14 years, my first wife and I called it quits. Actually, she called it quits. I was down on my knees, begging for mercy and forgiveness and even pleading for her not to take William away from me. She was not having it. Smart woman. I do not blame her. I would have left me, too. I failed her, my son, our families, friends and more. FAIL.

My second marriage lasted a year, barely. Go figure. Infidelity, overlap, tainted fruit with drama. Do you see a pattern? Our wedding was in the dark. Yes, outside at night. No guests. It never stood a chance. I was not present in that relationship either. What is worse is that our children were affected by all of this. Remember, our kids do what they SEE and not what we SAY. The space that my second wife and I were in was negative and unproductive. Both of us were suffering. Our kids were, too. I moved out. Failure again. A takeaway from all of my relationships is that we were not equally yoked. It is not just the physical that matters. The spiritual, emotional, and mental must be aligned as well.

Oh, and by the way, I filed for Chapter 7 bankruptcy, too. Going through this process, although painstakingly stressful, was extremely helpful for me. I had the option of entering all of my financials online or hiring an attorney. I chose Attorney Ronnie D. Slaven Jr., Esquire. He and his team of associates were great for me. This was right up my alley because all I was required to do was gather the information. It wasn't easy, but it still saved me a lot of time and frustration of trying to figure out all of the steps and details. Applying for bankruptcy over time finally allowed me to start over with a clean slate! When the dust finally settled, I still found myself sleeping on an air mattress in my best friend's home office, next to my son, William. They offered to put us up in the Westin Hotel, but I declined. I was grateful for his office. I told them, "I need to go through this. It hurts my heart that I am sleeping in my best friend's office at their home, with my son. I will never go through this again." And I never looked back.

Thinking back, I was failing long before marriage. At the Naval Academy, our strength coach, Phil Emery, was hassling me about working out. He emailed me all the players he helped get to the NFL.

Coach Phil was brewing with wisdom, but I believed I knew much more. Utter madness. This man later became the General Manager of the Chicago Bears and then went on to be director of scouting for the Kansas City Chiefs and Atlanta Falcons. Today, he is a scout for the Atlanta Falcons. Coach Phil knows football at the highest levels. This was my response to him:

"I run a 4.4-40, I was ALL ECAC Player of the Week last week, I had 3 interceptions and the game-saving tackle in the Toledo game in their beloved Glass Bowl, I had an endzone interception against Rick Mirer and Notre Dame in Giants Stadium, I was the leading interceptor on the team last year and on track to be Navy's all-time interceptor. I DON'T NEED TO WORKOUT."

This was fatal. He forwarded my email to my head coach and defensive backs coach. I WAS DONE. So, what is the moral of that story? Do not be COCKY, STUPID, BRAZEN, OBTUSE, IMMATURE or STUBBORN. PICK ONE. I was all of those things. ***Sometimes, the ones with the MOST TALENT make the MOST EGREGIOUS mistakes. Your talent will only get you so far. Remember?*** Are you wondering if things got worse? Yes indeed, they did. It was the first stage of failure.

Granted, it takes moxie to play my position well. However, I was exceptional at it, and I knew it. I played the wide-side cornerback position. Meaning, I was responsible for the largest area of the field. So, if I made a great play, then the world saw it, and if I made a bad play, then the world saw it. They say the greats have the shortest memories. I have no recollection of making any bad plays.

Except there was one play during practice when my collegiate football world went upside DOWN. I was already on thin ice. I tried to, stupid and arrogantly, intercept a pass by jumping over our tight end. Dumb. All I had to do was do the smart, right thing. Make the tackle! Nope. I went for the pick and dropped the ball, literally. "YANCEY! GET OFF OF THE FIELD! CHRIS HART, YOU'RE IN! You're our new starting cornerback." I was a rising senior. Chris Hart was a Plebe, a first-year student. Enough said.

What is the lesson? Whenever you think you know it all, YOU DON'T. YOU LOSE! **In the words of Thomas Jefferson, "He who knows best, knows how little he knows."** I failed to see the BIG PICTURE. *Failed to see my role individually as one of eleven players on the field and, more importantly, the example I was setting for those on the sidelines and beyond. I failed to look past myself and understand the value of TEAM. Nobody does it alone. NOBODY. Arrogance is a sneaky betrayer. It makes you believe that YOU can do it all by yourself, that you do not need A-N-Y-B-O-D-Y E-L-S-E. I WAS DEAD WRONG.*

I heard a quote by Aristotle, the Greek philosopher. **"THE WHOLE IS GREATER THAN THE SUM OF ITS PARTS,"** I recall my teacher evangelizing this EVERY DAY in geometry class! It was nauseating to me. I did not get the message. It took me years to finally understand and appreciate this quote. I learned that parts of me are really good, and I have parts that require more attention. However, in this, I also discovered that things I perceived as weaknesses were actually my strengths. It would take years for me to completely understand.

I realize now that the same applies to success and failure. Failure has value. Failure, if approached the right way, can be an asset. Failure is extremely valuable. **How?** Through our response. HOW we respond to failure is most important. We can win through failure.

Again, failure is your springboard OR your quicksand. Take your pick, UP or down. In this situation, along with others along the way, I chose quicksand. I chose down. **Today, I CHOOSE UP.** Either way, I stand before you today as the sum and failures of my life. I am a better version of myself. I encourage you to do the same. Choose UP. Do not be overconfident or arrogant. Be confident and assured. Do not cheat. Be fair. Do not lie. Be honest. **Do not fail. WIN!**

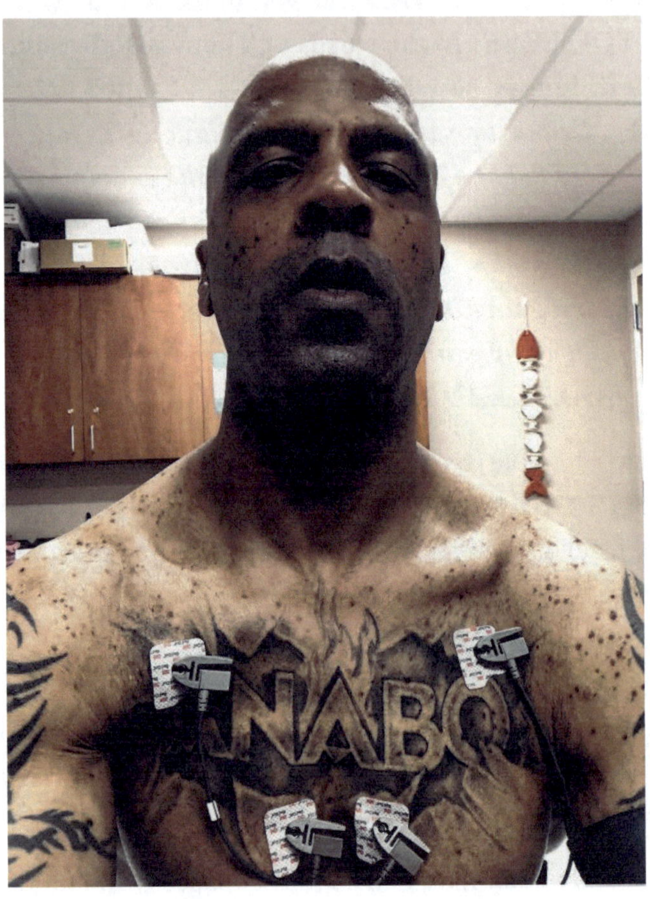

Chapter Six: Know It All

"The fear of the LORD is the beginning of knowledge, but fools despise wisdom and instruction."
Proverbs 1:7 NIV

In 2018, Virginia Beach, Hampton Roads, and the rest of the world lost one of the all-time greats, Al Walker. Al was strong, studied, witty, private, boisterous, serious, jovial, kind, and loving in his own "one-of-a-kind" way. I was introduced to Al in 1993 because I was interested in bodybuilding. I heard that if I wanted to get serious, then "Big Al is the man." My friend pointed him out to me at a local bodybuilding competition. The wall was leaning up against him. That's how big Al was. In conversation with a few folks, mouths shut while hanging onto every word, school was in session. Al was being Al. Light chatter, always sprinkled with a few nuggets of wisdom.

At the time, I knew nothing about Al. I had no idea that he had played Major League Baseball, traveled nationally, and played adult softball, or that he had trained and written nutrition plans for amateur, national, and professional competitors in all sports, even bodybuilding. All I saw was a big fat guy. I thought to myself, "how can this big fat dude help me be a bodybuilder?" Little did I know that this 350-lb round man would help carve me into the 2-time Mr. Virginia Bodybuilding Champion. After winning my first title, he shared, "you are the first here to ever receive a standing ovation after a posing routine… Wow." This was a huge honor. Yes, because it happened, but more so for me, because Al was in the audience and stood up and clapped as well. Me being elated is an understatement. I was pumped. I thought I was the stuff. That was a huge accomplishment, but few knew I had to see a therapist a few times before the competition. I was petrified to get on stage. But Big Al helped in this regard as well. "You worked hard. You earned it. Now get up there and have fun." That was Al. He was direct. He spoke in truth.

Al was renowned. Al was legendary. He showed and taught me how to work hard and how to work through pain. He brought things out of me I forgot I knew I had, as well as things I never knew I had. I will always remember challenging Al to a leg workout. Of all the tools he equipped me with, this particular one had the most profound effect on me. "Never play another man's game. Especially if you don't know the rules, you can't win. Do what you can do… not what someone else is doing." Basically, STAY IN YOUR LANE.

Welp. By the end of the workout, I was laying on my back, hyperventilating in front of BRUTUS. Brutus is a squat machine at Flex Gym that Al paid one of his friends to modify to his liking. The weight stack was 400-lbs, but that wasn't the problem. ***The problems were*** 1) weight could be stacked onto the rails that were attached to the sides, 2) Al had his friend add hydraulics to Brutus to increase drag and suffering 3) For this workout, Al added a few 45-lb plates to each side, 4) I was a jackass and demanded to lift the same weight he was doing. There I lay panting while Al stood over me with his giant hand hovering above my face, telling me to "relax and focus on my palm." This was almost like my little league football coach standing over me after Mike cleaned my clock in football practice. Complete humiliation. Yet in still another way for Guru, as he was also called, to navigate someone out of a fire storm they got themselves into. Lesson learned. We worked out together a few times following. I stayed in my lane.

Al explained to me in detail how certain things worked, why they worked, along with other things, and how and why they did not. Things being exercises, diets, methods, you name it. He seemed to know it all. IF, for some strange reason, he did not know, he'd just say, "I don't know. Never heard of it." It was that simple. I am sure many of you know those who claim to know everything. Not Al. He claimed what he knew and made a point of knowing it well.

I am a firm believer in, "that which can make you, can also break you." As I worked my way up the bodybuilding (food) chain, which wasn't very high, I got cocky. After all, I was the 2-time Mr. Virginia (1999, 2001). I had certain expectations. You know what I am getting at. ENTITLEMENT. I wanted what I wanted. It was my way or my way. That is how I saw things. Al thought otherwise.

One day, he asked me to sit down and have a conversation about what was bothering him, which was basically my attitude. There was no arguing, raising of voices, or anything remotely close to that. He said what he wanted to say, and I listened to every word intently. I never spoke. When he finished, I got up and walked out. We didn't utter a word to each other for 14 years. Really. After that one conversation, or lecture rather, as I saw it, we never made eye contact. Yup. None. I was ridiculously immature. I did not care for what he had to say. I could not process any of it. In my head, I was right, and he was unequivocally wrong.

It took me years to realize the opposite was correct. There are aspects of business that owners can appreciate, and independent contractors never understand. I was one of them. I was the one who was unequivocally wrong. I finally understood his frustration. It wasn't until I opened my own gym that it all made sense. A month after that last talk with Al, I packed up my toy box and started training at another gym. I was extremely immature. This was in 2001.

The next time I spoke to Al was at a friend's funeral in 2015. I walked up to him and said hello. We shook hands, and that was it. Never saw him in person again. Had not spoken more than two words ("Hello, Al") to him in over 14 years, then he died 4 years later. I did not go to his celebration of life.

Truth be told, I learned a lot from Al. He taught me how to train. He taught me that when I'm training someone, that being a cheerleader is not helpful. He said, "when a person is lifting weights, they need instruction for when it starts to get hard, and when they're in pain… you have to tell them what to do and how. None of this yelling and screaming crap." I listened. That stuck with me, which is one of the motivations for me writing my first book. So many of the younger generation need guidance for when things get difficult and when they are in pain. 'What they should do' and 'how to do it' is crucial. I'm here to help.

Despite the fallout with me and Al, there are lots of little nuggets I hung onto. If he gave you a nickname, he liked you. He called me Ball. I never knew why. If he yelled at you, "NO, DUMMY," or "WHAT DO YOU THINK, DUMMY." then he liked you a lot. I got called a dummy a lot over those 8 years.

I really looked up to Al. I recall a friend telling me one day that I really should tell him that I love him. I was like, "Huh? Tell Al I love him?" She insisted I tell him. She went on to say, "Come on, how many people do you think tell Big Al they love him?" "EXACTLY," I said. "Which is why you should," she finished. I intentionally caught Al outside one day, walked up to him, and said, "I love you, Al."

"WTF, get the hell away from me." "I do," I said. "Get the hell away from me, Ball." That was Al. I'm still glad I told him. Rest In Peace, Big Guy.

As I mentioned before, I attended an all-boy private school named Landon in Bethesda, MD. It required a pricey tuition we simply could not afford. Despite "interviewing very well" with Mr. Harrison Triplett, Landon's Headmaster at the time, and his insistence that we apply, my mother was obstinate. The tuition in 1978 was $4500. "There is no way we can afford that, Mr. Triplett," my mother exclaimed. "Just apply, please, Mrs. Yancey," he replied. Landon and Mr. Triplett made a way. They accepted me. Large financial aid contributions on their part, along with my parents' salaries and my mom working an extra job, paved the way to a tremendous education, along with priceless friendships I still have today. I am grateful for the generosity and the opportunity afforded by Landon.

Back then, I was not so appreciative. I begged my mother not to make me go to Landon. But, just like Mr. Triplett insisted that we apply, my mom insisted that I go. I was devastated. I had to repeat the 5th grade. I hated that because I thought my friends would joke me and call me stupid. I felt alone and unconfident, and I had to wear a coat and tie to school every day. Landon has a summer reading list that I hated, and there were only 63 kids in my graduating class, 60 of them Caucasian. The only other people of color on campus drove the school buses, managed the grounds, or worked in the kitchen. I felt outnumbered. My classmates were cool, **BUT** certain ones were mean. They made fun of how I talked and laughed at me. They were prejudiced, and I was tormented by them daily.

I took several public buses, the school bus, and walked a long way just to get *to and from* school. *It seemed everyone at Landon had expensive cars*: Mercedes Benz, BMW, Rolls Royce, etc. My mom drove a Toyota Corolla, and I eventually had a Volkswagen Super Beetle. I was embarrassed. To top it all off, *my classmates lived in HUGE HOUSES*. Compared to where I lived, my classmates lived in paradise. But, over time, I learned that *just because you have a lot of money doesn't mean you're rich, AND just because you're rich doesn't mean you have a lot of money*. Wisdom.

Over time, I adjusted to my classes, the dress code, and my haters. Deep down, if I was going to private school, I wanted to have an expensive car and live in a big fancy house. Neither ever happened.

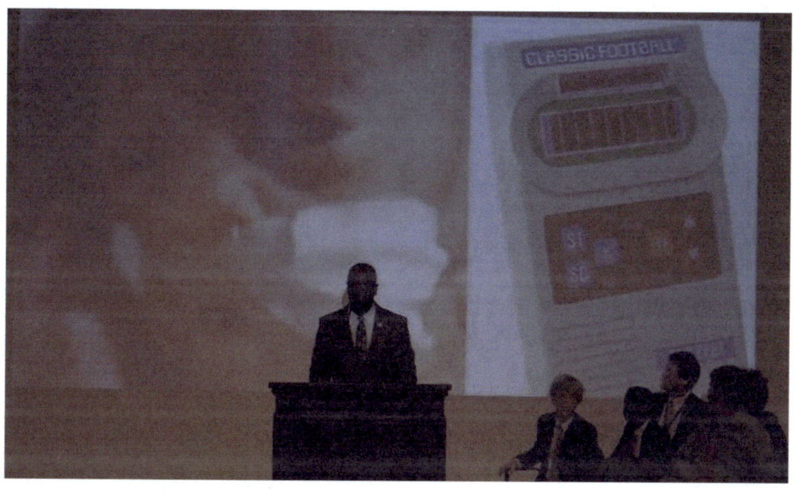

I'm sharing this experience with you to provide some context regarding opportunity. Without Mr. Triplett's insistence for us to apply to Landon, the opportunity to attend one of the most elite private schools, along with manifesting some of the most amazing friendships, would've never happened. THERE ARE FEW THINGS MORE VALUABLE THAN OPPORTUNITY. With opportunity, so many doors are opened, and dreams are realized. Without accepting Landon's offer in 1978, on June 5, 1987, I am not blessed with the esteemed honor of receiving the ***William Harrison Triplett Award*** for "team dedication, respect for opponents, and outstanding spirit in athletics."

Without attending Landon, I would not have been invited back 31 years later to be the keynote speaker and address the entire school and Landon community at the Landon School Chris Nelson Lecture Series. Without attending Landon, the Naval Academy probably would not have happened; I don't get stationed in Norfolk, Virginia, to finally meet William's mother in order to bring him into the world. So many things are achieved or unrealized with or without opportunity. Not all gifts are instant or unveiled overnight, so stop looking for instant gratification. I was once told, "Not all of God's gifts come wrapped in a pretty red bow." Meaning that all successes, accomplishments, or opportunities will not be delivered on a silver platter, perfectly created, designed, and fit to your liking and lifestyle. Thanks again, Sharon.

Case in point. I am not proud of this next share, but here it goes. Remember, this book is more about you than it is about me. About a month before I was to report to the Naval Academy Preparatory School, I went to a restaurant with a few friends to eat pizza. We were celebrating my nomination. It was good to catch up with the guys. Anyway, the idea comes up that we are going to walk out without paying. I have no idea why we decided this would be a good idea. Maybe because we were teenagers, bored, and wanted to do something dangerous. It was not because we couldn't pay for it. Our grand plan detailed one of my friends going into the bathroom and the other waiting at the table while I walked to get the car. I was the getaway guy. When I pulled up front, my friend waiting at the table was to get up and walk out. You can tell we are pros at this, right?

NOT SO MUCH.

So, I walk out to my car, pull up front, and then my guy sitting at the table comes busting out the front door, sprints to the car, and yells, "GO! GO! GO! GO! GO!" He freaked out sitting at the table, got antsy, and ran out. No one said anything to him. He just got spooked and ran out. I said, "Where's your cousin?" He's like, "What? I thought he already came out! Is he still inside?" Clearly, this was not a good idea. I drove around the block a few times looking for our buddy; all the while, we were both thinking that the police were on the way. A few minutes pass, and his cousin comes casually strolling out and gets in the car. 'WHAT HAPPENED?" we both asked. Evidently, our server was waiting outside of the bathroom for him when he walked out. He said, "Your boys ran out on you. Somebody needs to pay this bill." He paid the bill and walked out. If that was not one of the dumbest things I have EVER done, then it is a close second. I was raised not to lie, cheat, or steal. Yet, for some reason, for no reason at all, I tried stealing. Our plan failed. Or did it?

Let us break this down into the possibilities had THINGS GONE AWRY. Get arrested, go to jail, get my car impounded, parents bail me out (or not), deal with the wrath of mom, then dad, then mom again, hire attorney, go to court, await my fate, frowned upon at Landon, Naval Academy nomination GONE, never meet Lisa and create William, no Mr. Virginia, no Anabo, no no no no no!

I know. I know. I know. WHY ON EARTH WOULD I DO SOMETHING SO STUPID? Knowing my upbringing and the values ingrained into my brain, how could I even pander to the thought of leaving without paying? Why would I take a chance at risking and ruining my opportunity and future? The answer is, I don't know. My two friends are good guys as well. Both are living successful lives.

We were three good, young men who made a poor decision, but God. Again, I'm not proud of it. But that's what happened.

The lesson is to listen! Listen to what is being taught. You don't know it all. No one does. Not even you. Our parents, elders, teachers, counselors, and coaches have had a lot of experiences and have lots of wisdom. Don't even think about doing wrong. Do right! The short-term pleasures are not worth the long-term problems.

Chapter Seven: Fear!

**"Fear not, for I have redeemed you; I have called you by name,
you are mine."
Isaiah 43:1**

In 2004, when I left Flex, I needed a new place to train my clients.
I started working at a huge, brand-spanking *new gym on the block*,
BIG GYM. It was 25,000 sq-ft with all the bells and whistles. Two
brothers brought their BIG GYM concept down from Northern
Virginia, and it exploded. These guys were high energy,
knowledgeable, fit, handsome, cordial, and driven. They cleared out
an old grocery store in a Virginia Beach shopping center and filled it
with workout machines, treadmills, ellipticals, rowers, dumbbells,
TVs, aerobic classes, and members. There was nothing else in town
like BIG GYM. William's mother, Lisa, helped with their grand
opening and started working there on day one. She helped arrange my
interview, and the owners and staff welcomed me with open arms.

Although I was excited to get started, there was some angst. For
starters, BIG GYM is more than twice the size of Flex, and the layouts
were drastically different. Flex was also loaded with Hammer
Strength equipment, plate-loaded machines that targeted muscles
almost perfectly. This was my favorite equipment. All fitness levels
can use it, and it's extremely safe. It is unmatched. BIG GYM had no
Hammer Strength. This in itself was a major adjustment. It forced me
to resort to other alternatives.

Overall, workouts took more time to navigate between exercises.
Either I had to create new exercises and change up the order or take
more time and keep the order the same. Everything seemed longer,
the workouts and my days. I was out of sync. I lost my rhythm.

The differences created some uncertainty and doubt. You know the deal. Change is hard. In my head, "Did I make the right decision?" "Should I have stayed at Flex?" "Will my clients like BIG GYM?" "Will I get used to wearing the required red 'Personal Trainer' golf shirt?" "Will I, along with my clients, embrace and accept new pricing and contractual agreements?" "Will my clients stay or return to Flex?" "Will my clients leave Flex and come with me to BIG GYM?" I was scared everything was going to unravel.

Some of my clients came with me, while others chose not to. A couple of them came initially, then returned to Flex. One came to visit BIG GYM, walked in, and knew right away, "Nah, this place is too big. It's huge. This would give me anxiety. I'm so sorry. I can't do it." There were a lot of things I had to work through mentally. It was painfully stressful.

As I shared earlier, the busiest nights in the gym business tend to be on Mondays. After the weekend, people want to detox from the last 48-72 hours! During this Monday afternoon, I was training one of my clients, a young lady named Justyn. We were in the thick of the rush-hour madness. Crowded, loud, members waiting on machines, etc. I was spotting Justyn while she was doing chest flys. One of the rules of the gym was being blatantly ignored. A big sign was posted in the dumbbell area: **DO NOT DROP THE DUMBBELLS.**

("BOOM BOOM!")

A few minutes go by…

("BOOM BOOM!")

I look across the gym and see two guys lifting heavy dumbbells and then dropping them to the floor at the end of each set. Although the rows of dumbbells lined up against a wall, most were unaware of that space being an old loading dock for groceries. What was once part of a ramp enclosed with huge metal grates for tractor-trailers was now a framed gymnasium with glossy paint-covered drywall, giant sparkly windows, and rubber floor matting. Even when a lighter dumbbell hit the floor in that area, the sound would reverberate throughout the gym. All 25,000 feet. These two were lifting and *intentionally* dropping 80-lb dumbbells on a hollow floor. **IT WAS LOUD.**

They were about 100 feet away from me and Justyn. Despite the crowd, talking, yelling, grunting, laughing, loud music pumping, treadmills, and ellipticals racing, and classes jumping up and down, we could still hear these two knuckleheads slamming the weights. Let us call them Tall Guy and Short Guy. I bet you can't guess why. These two were a piece of work. They would do a few sets, look in the mirror, stroll around the gym, find another mirror, stop-flex-smile, and then stroll some more before starting their next exercise. They were actually pretty funny to watch. They reminded me of the old me, yester-me. But this Monday afternoon, I was not laughing.

Waving my arms and displaying the Luigi death stare, I was able to get their attention, motioning for them to stop dropping the dumbbells. **They would not stop.** I know they heard me, so I signaled once more. **AND THEN**, Short Guy turns, looks at me, stretches his little arms up into the air, and flips me the DOUBLE BIRD. Oh no he didn't. Justyn and I look at each other, mouths dropped. She knew IT WAS ON THEN.

Me: Excuse me, Justyn. I'll be right back.

Justyn: No, no, no, Billy. Please don't go over there. Just stay here, pleasssssse.

Me: I'll be fine. Be right back. This won't take long.

I make a beeline for Short Guy and Tall Guy, in that order. Short Guy made me mad. I had my BIG BOY WALK on. I can't tell you how fast I made it across the gym. FAST. A small crowd gathers. They know tension had been mounting. I walked up to Short Guy.

Me: WHAT DID YOU SAY TO ME? (Me and Short Guy were almost nose to nose!)

He stretches his little arms back in the air... DOUBLE BIRD, again. I stepped up closer to him.

Me: THAT'S IT. YOU TWO ARE OUT.

I stormed away to my Personal Training manager's office, just knowing it was only a matter of moments before Tall Guy and Short Guy would be escorted out. I explained the whole scenario, and he said he would take care of it. I went back to finish up Justyn's workout.

A few minutes later, I see my manager walk over to Tall Guy and Short Guy, expecting the grand exit. The next thing I know, my PT manager's walking over to me. The knuckleheads are still working out, mind you. WHAT IS GOING ON? My manager walks up and says,

PT Manager: I talked to them. They said they will keep it down.

Me: They said they will keep it down? Did you hear anything I said? They punked you. This is some bull, man. The little one flipped me off in front of the whole gym, TWICE. And they were in the wrong. They need to go.

I WAS HOT. It took me a while to calm down from that.

The next day, the club manager was sitting in his office. I walked in and closed the door.

Club Manager: What's up Billy… what's going on?"

Me: You hear what happened last night? Tall Guy and Short Guy were at it again. This time, they went off the rails. Short Guy, mostly.

Club Manager: No way. What?

Me: Yup. Little punk flipped me off last night when I told them to stop dropping the weights. I told them a few times. Nope. DOUBLE BIRDED ME. This place was packed.

Club Manager: Whoaaaaa. Double birded you? Why didn't you call me? I would've come up.

Me: Come on man. I am not bugging you on your day off over some stuff that can be handled in house. It is just crazy that it played out like that. I was fired up!

Club Manager: I bet! That never should've happened. I'll take care of it. Thanks for telling me.

Well, the image of Tall Guy and Little Guy being escorted out of the gym that night never happened, but they did, in fact, get suspended. They weren't allowed back for a month. YES! Served them right.

That incident never sat well with me. I had finally gotten over the fear and uncertainty of leaving the gym I was a part of for 8 years (Flex) and now settled at BIG GYM. My client base eventually stabilized and even increased. At the crux of the Tall Guy, Short Guy incident was *respect*. I was doing my job, asked them to stop breaking a rule, confronted them, and was disrespected in the interim. It felt even worse because it happened in front of so many people. Two members, doing what they want, how they want, wherever they want with zero accountability. In the end, I had no support from my Personal Training manager. How does that work? It didn't for me. That was the beginning of the end.

The closest I came to feeling this betrayed actually happened at Flex. I phoned a client to remind him that he needed to renew his sessions with me before his next workout. I'll never forget it. A few hours later, while me, Al, and a few other Flex staff members were talking at the front counter, my client walked into the gym. I walked over and greeted him. As he pulled out a balled-up check from his pocket, he threw it on the counter and said, "Don't aggravate me," and then he walked out. You talk about heated. Al and the whole group busted out laughing, giving me the business. Major humiliation. A girl I was dating probably gave me the best advice. She said, "You know what…I get it. It sucks, right? He embarrassed you in front of your crew, and you know what, you got paid. You honor it. Now, the next 12 sessions may be the hardest he has ever seen, and you may punish him, but hey, you got paid, and you are honoring the agreement. When it is over, you have the choice of continuing or not."

And that is exactly what I did. I honored the agreement. Were the next 12 sessions the hardest he experienced? Yes. Did I punish him? YES. Was his 12th session his last training with me? **YES!**

In both situations, I was embarrassed in front of a group. The difference at Flex was that I had a voice in the conversation. I was disrespected, and I retaliated on my own terms. At BIG GYM, it felt like I capitulated, which was extremely unsettling.

I left BIG GYM after two years. The newness had worn off, and I was on a different fitness path. The facility is superb, and I got the opportunity to work with a great group of people. It just was not a good fit for me.

One of my client's family businesses had a commercial space for rent. Apparently, it was an old bar open from 6 am to 2 am every day for over 30 years. The owner died, but his children didn't want the responsibility. It was called the London Bridge Inn, LBI. I could visit at any time to take a look at it. Although I really didn't know what to expect, I was anxious! I had a break after one of my afternoon clients, so I went to check it out.

It was not what I expected. It was very dark, cluttered, and so small. Almost claustrophobic. I walked from front to back, taking all 1500 sq-ft in. By the time I returned to the front, I had my mind made up, "I'll take it. Take the FOR-RENT sign down, please. It is mine."

I went home to Lisa and was so excited to share it with her. She said,

Lisa: Cool, we can talk about it later.

Me: I already told them I want it.

Lisa: You what?

Me: Yeah, I need to move on. I wanna do my own thing.

Lisa: We haven't even really talked about it. I know we discussed getting your own place, but there's a lot to it. I'm not trying to spoil your dream. I'm just saying it's a lot.

I had no idea HOW MUCH "a lot" was when she said it. I don't think she knew either, but Lisa definitely was more aware of the steps and details that I was oblivious to. I still remember the look on her face when I showed her the place.

Lisa: What the hell!

Me: I know it looks crazy in here, but I can do it. I have a vision.

Lisa: (Laughing) You better! Are you sure? We haven't even looked at other places, Billy. This place is a wreck. Do you know how much work this is gonna take?

Me: This is the place. This is it! WAYNE-O FIVE-O can help me.

Lisa walked out shaking her head, laughing.

Lisa: I can't believe you want this place. It's a dump! But, ok.

Words cannot describe how right Lisa was. I had no idea the magnitude of what I was trying to accomplish. I had absolutely zero business acumen. I only knew how to train people, get them in better physical shape, and improve their health. I knew nothing about commercial leasing agreements, bookkeeping, marketing, quarterly taxes, yearly business registration, yearly Fire Marshal inspections, pricing, how to get customers in the door, and so much more.

In 2004, we signed a three-year lease. A mountain's worth of work needed to be accomplished just to open the doors. First, LBI had been here since the 70s, so massive demolition and renovations would have to take place to bring the property up to code. The front and rear entry/exit points were absurdly narrow; the bathrooms were the size of a coat closet, a shower, and new toilets needed to be installed; there were three layers of paneling on the walls behind which cigarette and cigar smoke had been trapped for who knows how long. I do not have a good word for what that smelled like. Stench is probably the closest. We had to raise the ceiling and install new ceiling tiles and light fixtures, along with a new HVAC system. We also replaced the two and only windows in the whole building. One of them was boarded up. A car crashed through it years prior, so they just patched it up and kept rolling, I guess. Also, the bar, sinks, and ovens all needed to be removed. Every wall, aside from the four exteriors, had to come down. Yours truly, my buddies Big T and Wayne-O Five-O did the bulk of the demolition. It seemed like the pile would never get smaller. We started excavating in November and officially opened for business in February. Another buddy, Jeffie contributed majorly over the years by being my 'Mr. Fix It' for whatever needed attention. When we finally opened, I would work all day at BIG GYM, then go straight to my new place and work late into the night. This went on for 90 days. It was BRUTAL.

None of this was possible if not for my late friend, Wayne Speelman. He is responsible for all of the renovations. Everything! I called him Wayne-O Five-O, which had nothing to do with his work or work ethic. I just thought it was cool. He was an amazing friend, dad, husband, and human. Gigantic in heart, love, and spirit. He was one of the calmest, most giving people I have ever known. Wayne was insanely gifted at everything he did. Despite the endless compliments he received, Wayne was extremely humble. He always seemed to be even-keeled, never to the left or right, but always straight down the middle. I never heard him talk badly about anyone. Even if I said, "You know so and so is a real jerk," or if a person wronged him, then Wayne would clench his jaws, nod his head slightly, and barely mumble, "Hmm." Then he'd crack a smile and move on. That was it! Wayne was love personified. His specialty was his hands. Whether it was landscaping, painting, laying tile, installing drywall, or ceiling tiles, spraying our entire space with Kilz, or building his tricked-out Mustang, Wayne was deliberate, precise, and efficient. He always finished the job well. Everything he put his hands on was completed at the highest level.

Wayne was diagnosed with a rare form of cancer at age 34. He battled it for 10 years without a word or complaint that anything was wrong. That was Wayne. He died at age 44. The last time I saw him, he and his wife, Cheryl, stopped by the gym to say hello. We talked about him getting back into the gym the following week. He told me they were headed to a doctor's appointment for a check-up. I remember Cheryl texting me from the hospital, saying something was wrong with Wayne. He was not doing well. They did not know what was going on. I told her I would come by and see him later after I closed.

I locked up and drove straight to Wayne's house. I recall being really anxious, praying he was ok. I parked and walked up to the front door. There was a young lady sitting on the porch. I told her I came by to see Wayne and that I was texting with Cheryl a few hours before.

"I am so sorry, sir. Wayne never came home. He passed at the hospital."

I got back in my truck, drove down the street, and cried. I missed my friend. I felt horrible that I didn't go to the hospital. I thought he was ok. I had just talked to him earlier that day. He was coming in for a workout next week. He was fine. Wayne had come by the gym to say goodbye.

Finally, opening day had arrived. I was so excited. There I sat in my brand-new place with shiny new and used equipment, a refrigerator loaded with protein shakes, a counter full of supplements, a few TVs mounted, some treadmills, ellipticals, bikes, and a three-year lease agreement, by myself.

Was I scared? 100%! I had a number of people "say" they were coming to work out when I opened my new place. Most never came. A few of my clients came with me. Others either stayed at BIG GYM, went back to Flex, or I never heard from them again.

Although I believed that I thought it all through, I did not. I went from one gym with moderate traffic, to a much larger gym with heavy traffic, to my gym with no traffic. It all came crashing down at once. I cannot tell you how many days I sat in my gym, from open (5 am) to close (9 pm), 7 days/week BY MYSELF. Eventually, I had a few newspaper and radio ads, some television and radio interviews, along with some gorilla marketing, putting fliers on parked cars, and door-to-door businesses.

These were all ok, but I made the largest impact by riding an old stationary bike on the sidewalk, right in front of my gym. The motive was to announce, HEY! LOOK! THIS IS A NEW GYM OVER HERE! Countless passersby honked their horns, waved, yelled "HELLO," and stopped by to acknowledge some strange guy riding a stationary bike every day during rush hour. IT WORKED! Today, 17 years later, I still have people talking about "the guy riding a stationary bike out front." I've had a number of gym members and clients sign up because of my gorilla bike riding.

As I approach my 20th year in business, with a plethora of peaks and valleys along the way, and although many times I did not know HOW, I've always had faith that, one way or another, IT WOULD ALL WORK OUT. I have stressed, lost sleep, and cried like a baby to my best friend, David, but I have never said I quit. I have had my water and power cut off and paid bills late, but I never said no mas.

At the core of all my mishaps, breakdowns, and frustrations was FEAR. The fear of leaving the gym where I trained and grew my reputation as a trainer for eight years, the fear of not being able to succeed at a new gym, the fear of opening my own gym, the fear of not being able to pay my rent, the fear of my utilities being cut off, the fear of going on vacation and not having any clients when I returned, the fear of failure.

In my business, people want results. They want to see a difference in themselves. They want to know and trust that they are getting the most out of their money, effort, and time. If I have a fear of money, a fear of effort, and a fear of time, then I am providing a disservice. I cannot give what I don't have. I cannot effectively and rightfully coach or encourage what I cannot manage in my own mind.

I have learned to be fearless, resolute. Regardless of circumstances, situations, or complications, there is nothing I cannot work through, figure out, or solve. The same goes for you. There is no problem you cannot solve or issue you cannot resolve. Fear will shake or stir you. Do not allow it to stop you. "Too many of us are not living our dreams because we are living our fears." -Les Brown.

Chapter Eight: Goals!

**"Commit to the Lord whatever you do, and He will establish
your plans."
Proverbs 16:3**

I have always had huge goals. From yearning to attend and graduate from the Naval Academy, then serve as a Naval officer, to wanting to be Mr. Virginia, to striving to create and build the greatest digital fitness program in the universe ever. With huge goals comes massive resistance. I could write a book on resistance alone. Whatever your goals, you will always have friends, family, customers, acquaintances, accomplices, and strangers who will not only disagree but will also try to dismantle them. It took me a while to learn, embed, and practice the mantra, "What you think of me is none of my business." In other words, I DO NOT CARE WHAT YOU THINK ABOUT MY GOALS. Better yet, I DON'T CARE WHAT YOU THINK ABOUT ME. A lot of people think lowly of themselves, or not as highly as you, and want you to jump on the struggle bus with them. NOPE. Not an option. That is not happening. There are also those who are just plain mean and genuinely do not want good fortune for anyone but themselves.

I have had doses of them all. Upon entering the Naval Academy Preparatory School and the United States Naval Academy, I had upper-class on both campuses trying to run me out. It is one thing for the powers that be to try and weed out the weak, but it's another to target athletes, particularly football players, and make our lives a living hell. You already know I was ambushed a number of times by upperclassmen during Plebe Summer.

Chow calls are part of the tradition at the Naval Academy. They serve three purposes: 1) alert the company of the menu for the upcoming meal, 2) remind upperclassmen and the rest of the company of the minutes remaining before formation, 3) humiliate the plebes. Usually, there are only two sets of chow calls. One at ten minutes before formation and another five minutes before formation. The plebe giving the chow call, screaming a litany of information at the top of their lungs for thirty seconds out in the hallway, is a sitting duck. Literally, everyone can hear them, and all of the upperclassmen are listening for mistakes. Upperclassmen are waiting for a plebe to stumble, stammer, repeat words, forget an item, say something wrong, or anything. It is already tense. The saving grace of the ten and five-minute chow calls is said plebe dashing into a nearby room between chow calls, out of sight of lurking upperclassmen.

The deal is, they don't have to sit and wait out in the hallway, which can be problematic, UNLESS they are on All-calls. This is a whole different animal. With All-calls, you do not get to disappear into a nearby room. You have to stand out in the hallway, at the mercy of whomever, and give a chow call at the start of every minute. Once you hear that clock "CLICK," you better be yelling or else.

Well, yours truly was on All-calls right outside the room of this jerk senior who despised football players, me. I didn't care for him either, but I was a plebe, and he was not. Anyway, I was giving my chow call and got stuck. All 5ft-6 of him comes out of his room and invades my space. I am 5ft-11, so there is already a problem. The Napoleon complex is in full effect. He was barking, barking, barking, barking, and I started leaning towards him because I had had enough of his little self. Saved by the bell. Another company mate who outranked him happened to come out, saw what was about to happen, and shoved me off. "Shoved me off," meaning he gave me an order that I was clear to leave. This guy was on the swim team. He rescued me, knowing Little Napoleon was just being an ass. Upper-class Swimmer guy did not have to do this, of course, and I was grateful beyond measure. This is an example of a bitter person attempting to get someone else to come down to their level. But his plan was thwarted. No one knows what would have transpired if the Upper-Class Swimmer guy had not excused me. Little Napoleon and I could have been in fisticuffs, and my Academy and Naval Officer goals would have gone up in smoke.

When I started taking weight-lifting more seriously, I grew to like and appreciate bodybuilding. I liked the results possible from the hard work, and I had an appreciation for the discipline required to obtain those results. Like other parts of me, I became obsessed with it. Not only did I want to have the best body. I wanted to be Mr. Virginia. This would take an unimaginable amount of work, time, discipline, and dedication. Once I came to the realization that claiming the title was possible, I knuckled down and went all in.

It took me back to a conversation I had with another jerk. His name was Drew. He was this huge bodybuilder, always eating tuna out of a can, plain chicken breast, and white rice, with a jug of water in tow. Actually, it was not even a conversation. He just went off on me in this café next to the gym we used to go to. It was 100% unprovoked. Maybe he was just having a bad day. I don't even remember how it started, but he said,

"You will never be a bodybuilder, you little f*#k! Are you kidding me? You look like a tennis player! Look at your skinny little legs.

You look like you run track! You ran track, didn't you? Give it up, f*#kin pu@3y!"

I said nothing. Hands down, one of the most humiliating moments of my life. I didn't know how to feel and sure didn't know what to say. How could I refute any of it? All I knew was that I was being terrorized by this dude that I wanted to be as big as, if not, bigger. He was a huge bodybuilder, and I was a guy who lifted weights, who used to run track and play tennis competitively, but I did not tell him that. This huge bodybuilder is screaming at me, the former tennis player and track star, that I couldn't be a bodybuilder. I didn't know whether to believe him or not. What was I going to say? He was a bodybuilder, and I was not. In any event, I never forgot the grilling Drew gave me. Ultimately, that was fuel for the fire that he helped start. The same venom Drew spit at me, I used to motivate me and supercharge my workouts. I was Mr. Virginia not just once BUT TWICE.

Going forward, little did I know but I would not just be a two-time state bodybuilding champion. I would also eventually have my own gym. Despite the long, arduous road of entrepreneurship, I have a thriving business. I chose the name **ANABO** because, unlike most programs, all we need is a *spark* to strengthen our bodies. **ANABO** means "ignite" in Greek. One brief action starts a chain reaction.

In 2011, **ANABO** was born from a few workouts on a whiteboard. Today, it is a *fitness technology company* for all fitness levels, kids, adults, seniors, and professional athletes. **ANABO** works by strengthening your mental toughness. Remember, it is more challenging to complete a task ***under pressure*** in a fixed amount of time. **ANABO** entails doing various exercises ***under pressure*** for different spans of time.

Early in **ANABO**'s infancy, I received some pushback from a few people. A couple were close friends of mine. The first one questioned, "What if someone takes your idea and opens up down the street from you? What are you gonna do then? It does not make a whole lot of sense to me."

A few things here. If I approached business with that attitude, then I would not have the success I have today. You cannot play scared or worry about 'who's doing what' down the street. I do not compete against anybody but MYSELF. And, lastly, this friend said, "…It does not make a whole lot of sense to me." Of course, it did not make sense to him. It was not his vision. He is in the trucking industry. What would he know about creating a fitness technology company, and why would I listen to him? Hmmm.

Another friend really liked my vision but encouraged me to sell it to a company on the West Coast. He said, "My buddy, George, is an attorney out there. He works with that company. I'm sure he can arrange a meeting for you." I replied, "**IT'S NOT FOR SALE!**"

My best friend, David, was the most perplexing, yet meaningful. I recall a conversation with him as I walked into a grocery store 10 years ago. I was afraid that someone or some big company was going to take my idea, dump a bunch of money into it, leaving us high and dry. David assured:

David: You don't have to worry about that, Billy.

Me: Huh? What are you talking about? This has never been done. This will change fitness!

David: It is too hard, Billy. There is too much work. Nobody will take your idea because it is too hard. Nobody wants to do the amount of work that it will take to build this.

Me: Oh…ok

Today, while we build the **ANABO APP**, I fully understand what David, my best friend, was talking about. He was exactly right. This is more than I ever imagined. Our developers, as experienced as they all are, and we have the cream of the crop, have NEVER built anything close to what we are constructing. So many people jump on the bandwagon and tout, "We will change the world." My team and I are not that ambitious. Our mission is to help you make a small change inside yourself, individually. Small changes can make monumental gains.

In **ANABO,** thirty seconds is equivalent to one brick, one building block. What kind of body do you want to build? Remember, life is lived in seconds and minutes. Not reps and sets. Know and understand that constructing a durable, fit body one brick at a time, thirty seconds at a time, bolsters your foundation from the inside out. Along with proper nutrition, focusing on the individual seconds and minutes of your exercise will add strength to your mind, body, and years to your life. **ANABO** will change your fitness.

It takes more than a few minutes to learn life's lessons and achieve our goals. It took me fifty years to learn how to be 50 years old. Our society encourages instant gratification and Faustian behaviors, which over time, can be crippling. I discourage this highly. Respect the process and make every minute count in life and sport.

Owning a business is no cakewalk. Yes, I get to set my own hours, holidays, and vacations, which are infrequent, **BUT** I also get to work fourteen-hour days and open on time whether I am sick or not.

Riding the highs of a successful business is great. Enduring the lows are awful but surmountable. Hard times even forced me to sleep at the gym for weeks. Not something I am proud of, BUT I made it through. I won the battle. I went from almost closing my business for good, to being recognized as one of the top three gyms in Hampton Roads. This is just the beginning. **ANABO** is a worldwide brand weaving its way to billions of people everywhere.

The **ANABO formula** strengthens the mind and body altogether. Working through physical pressure makes you stronger mentally and physically. Training in this fashion increases your core strength, muscular strength, stamina, and mental toughness. It makes you fitter and tougher in minutes, literally. You get more bang for your buck, AND **YOU STOP WASTING TIME.** All fitness levels benefit because the workouts are designed specifically for them. By adhering to the *6-week progression protocol*, the body has time to grow, recover, avoid overtraining, and minimize downtime.

Some will argue that resistance training, reps, and sets, alone is the answer. But that has never resonated well with me. I have grown to understand and acquire a different perspective. Since everything is time-sensitive, then why don't we prepare for them in the same manner? Millions have nine-to-five jobs, and the **NBA** has a twenty-four-second clock. Strikingly, we have time zones throughout the world to help us stay on time, yet we carry on as if time never stops. *It is more challenging to complete a task under **pressure** in a fixed amount of time than it does to complete the same task at your leisure.* Most people know and believe this; however, when it comes to exercise, many choose the reps and sets format. Whether it is doing squats, sprints, or solving problems in math class, the intensity increases once the task is timed. Remember how pressured you felt the last time you heard, "Pencil's down?" It only takes one snap to start a football game and one tip-off to start a basketball game. **ANABO** is based on time because time is boss.

ANABO is the game changer. 30 seconds is the building block. The effort you put into each 30-second block yields huge benefits. Build brick by brick. With good eating habits along with sound effort during each 30-second block, results are guaranteed. We have hundreds of success stories from members and clients, as well as our 2016 Case Study that our system is proven. **ANABO** works. What are your goals? Life happens in seconds and minutes, not reps and sets. Without a doubt, resistance training improves strength. However, **ANABO** is more dynamic. The mind and body, as a cohesive unit, learn to work together for blocks of time, facing the pain and grinding through the pressure.

Studies show that exercise releases endorphins, which increase one's sense of well-being. I encourage you to incorporate some form of sustained physical activity into your daily routine. You do not have to be a bodybuilder, football player, fighter, or participate in any kind of organized athletics. This is specifically for YOU. For you to take care of yourself, maintain good health, and enjoy a vigorous life. I played tennis for many years and enjoyed it immensely. I still play occasionally. Tennis is fun, light, only requires one other person, and can be played leisurely or competitively. If you prefer not to participate in sports, then going for a walk or jog is beneficial. You will be amazed at how good you feel during and following light exercise. It will take your mind off of the pressure building up inside of you, burn excess calories, help eliminate body fat, increase your energy, and improve your cardiovascular system. My favorite side effect of exercise is euphoria or "natural high," many experts talk about. It is a great feeling. You must try it. It feels good to feel good. Would you agree?

Do not be afraid to set high goals and beware of the dream snatchers. People will try to dissuade your goals and crush your dreams. Do not let them. Stand fast. Stay true to your dreams. Believe in yourself! Hey! We only get one body, so it is best we take care of it while we're still here. Exercise. Get off of the couch and get moving! Like my mother and Clyde often say, "If nothing changes, then nothing changes." If you want to feel better, look better, move better, be healthier, reduce stress, and or improve your well-being, then you gotta move! LET'S GO! MOVE!

Chapter Nine: Drive!

"That is why, for Christ's sake, I delight in weaknesses, in insults, in hardships, in persecutions, in difficulties. For when I am weak, then I am strong."
2 Corinthians 12:10

Are you a pretender? I was. Are you pretending? I did. Are you saying one thing and doing another? Yes, I did that too. Come on, you know what I am talking about. Here is an example. Although I have heard it countless times from clients over the years, I remember this particular instance when my client was not doing what we agreed upon. After a few weeks, I asked him how the diet was going. He said,

Client: Billy, I am following it to a 'T'. I am doing everything you told me to do. I swear.

Me: You are eating all of your meals that I wrote down? No more, no less? Just drinking water?

Client: Yessir. Exactly what you told me. I don't know why this weight will not come off.

Me: What did you eat for lunch today?

Client: (He smiles) I went to Wendy's.

Me: (I smile back) Why are you smiling? What did you eat at Wendy's?

Client: I had a bacon cheeseburger, fries, and a Coke. I forgot my lunch at home. I have been doing good other than that. You know I am all in.

Pretender? Some of you may say he is straight-up lying. Well, what if he truly thinks he is "ALL IN?" He might 100% believe that he is doing everything right, all that he needs to do to get results. Others might say, "Well, he is doing the best he can." What if the best he can IS NOT ENOUGH? This is the reality. He IS NOT doing what he is supposed to do in order to get the results he seeks, nor is he doing *the best he can*, and furthermore, he is NOT ALL IN. If he were ALL IN, doing what he is supposed to be doing and doing the best that he can, then he would have the results. Period.

Sometimes, I think people are pretending and do not even know it. I used to be a pretender. The difference was that I knew I was pretending. I was not just pretending. I was a fraud. Yes, 100%. Spiritually, I was pretending. I was going to church worshiping God every Sunday, and sometimes during the week, AND THEN bathing in sin. Some of the habits I had, some of the friends I had, some of the clients I had, some of the things I read, some of the things I watched, some of the things I did, SINFUL. Meanwhile, I was praising God. I was fooling a lot of people. Guess who I was not fooling? God and me. That proved to be life-altering. You already know a lot of the despondency I experienced. I deserved every bit of it. My pretend habits were not just immersed in my spiritual life. They were ubiquitous.

I recall several years earlier pretending I was a bodybuilder. I was going to the gym religiously. I was at the gym four days in a row; then, I would take a day off. Eventually, I increased it to five days in a row. I believed I was right around the corner from bodybuilder fame and fortune. When ephedrine was the "in thing," I was all about it. Back then, ephedrine could be purchased at gas stations. Life was good. The recommended dosage was one-25mg tablet. One time, I TOOK FIVE! Yes, at the same time. I was not pretending to be a jackass, though. I was a jackass through and through! I had a great workout but did not sleep one minute that night. It felt like my heart was coming through my chest. It is no wonder I didn't have a heart attack. I marvel at the stupid things I have done that I survived. God is merciful.

All the while, I was pretending that I was a bodybuilder. I was lifting weights. I toted a gallon water jug around with me everywhere I went. I did the workouts I saw in the bodybuilder magazines. I started eating tuna right out of the can. I ate white rice and dry chicken breast. I was a bodybuilder, right? Not even close. You are not a bodybuilder until you diet for twelve to sixteen weeks, get your pump and oil on backstage, step under the lights, position next to competitors, muscle and grunt through prejudging mandatories, diet and dehydrate for another several hours, and finally battle your way through your 90-second posing routine. Then and only then are you a bodybuilder. I was not, yet. I was a pretender.

What does all of this have to do with *DRIVE*? When you are driven, a bacon cheeseburger, fries, and a Coke is not an option. When you are driven, you either DRIVE BY Wendy's or drive-thru Wendy's and get a salad and water. When you are driven, your faith is not compromised. When you are driven, your spiritual compass is not in your pocket. It is in your heart. Compartmentalizing nefarious behaviors is impossible. Guess where my spiritual compass was. I was clueless! I was not aware of a spiritual compass. Despite not being aware of my spiritual compass, I was driven negatively. How, you ask? It is said that one who is driven, is one who has a goal and refuses to be altered.

I had a goal and refused to be altered. But my focus was not on winning. My focus was on not losing. For my first Mr. Virginia competition, I was fixated on not slouching on stage, not forgetting to keep my shoulders down, not forgetting to keep my rib cage up, not forgetting to start my posing from the floor up, not forgetting to blow out all the air for my overhead abdominals pose, and not forgetting to smile. I paid for a few sessions with a psychiatrist because I was so worried about getting up on stage and messing up. I was driven not to mess up. That is exhausting. I won, but I expended way more energy and mental strength than I should have.

I digress. When one practices a certain craft for an extended amount of time, one develops habits, knowledge, and nuggets of wisdom about the craft. One knows what works and what does not. In the fitness industry, the ones *WHO KNOW* understand you cannot EXERCISE OFF body fat. A person loses body fat by adjusting his or her eating habits. It is what you do not eat that makes the largest impact! Now, I know someone out there is thinking, "I weighed three pounds less after my workout." That is not body fat. That is water weight. Question. What weighs more? 5-lbs of fat or 5-lbs of muscle? I cannot tell you how many times I have heard, "Muscle weighs more than fat." Negative! It does not! Here is the answer. NEITHER. 5-lbs is 5-lbs is 5-lbs is 5-lbs. 5-lbs of muscle takes up less space than 5-lbs of fat, so you will look smaller and firmer when you shed 5-lbs of body fat.

Resistance training (weightlifting) helps shape and strengthen the body, build muscle, and, in turn, create a fat-burning environment. The key is to avoid foods that feed the fat. Why? BECAUSE WEIGHTLIFTING CANNOT UNDO WHAT YOU DID AT THE TABLE. If you do not change your eating habits, then weight training will just make you a stronger, firmer, fatter version of yourself. It took me a few minutes to wrap my head around that, too. Therefore, is the argument that "I work out so that I can eat whatever I want" a myth? ABSOLUTELY, 100% MYTH! You can eat whatever you want, **BUT** to attain the results you yearn for, adjustments to your nutrition are required. The more change you want, the more discipline is required. These are the facts.

Just like I learned the truth about weight training and what it can and cannot do, results are a product of ***what we choose not to eat*** and not from the actual exercises. I also stumbled upon another truth. ___It is not necessary to work out for more than 30 minutes in one session.___ I mean, you can, but it is not necessary. That is correct. I figured it out. I cracked the code. First, I created an eighteen-minute workout, and it was challenging. Then, I morphed it into 9 minutes, and it kicked my butt. There I lay, flat on my back, completely wiped out in nine minutes. Mister Football, Mister Cornerback, and Mister Virginia, flattened in nine minutes. I called it the Shock9. I introduced it to a few of my close friends who were absolute gym rats, and it kicked their butts, too. All body parts, trashed in minutes. They loved it. I'll never forget my buddy, Toni, said after meeting the Shock9, "Man, what the hell was that? That is TV-ready. No joke. For real."

I knew I was onto something, so I kept at it. I found that many are sold on the sets and reps routine. You know, 3 sets of 10 reps of bench press, or 2 sets of 8 reps of squats, and blah blah blah. Set after set after set, and so on and so on. It never stops. But I figured it out. Most focus on "how much" when the answer lies in *"for how long."*

By basing our program on time and not sets and reps, I broke the mold of the fitness industry. What many deem the traditional workout, I tossed out the door. Really. Originally, my gym, Face the Pain Gym, was loaded with treadmills, bicycles, ellipticals, workout machines, and dumbbells. I got rid of everything except the dumbbells and benches. Every last one. I created an assortment of workouts: five-minute, seven-minute, nine-minute, twelve-minute, and eighteen-minute. Thirty-minute workouts: core, full body, cardio, split-training, various intensities. You name it. I was DRIVEN.

The next thing I knew, I had created a workout program for people of all ages and different fitness levels. From age 11 to 92. Remember, one who is driven, is one who has a goal and refuses to be altered. **ANABO was born.** Some of you are thinking, "What kind of drive, OR STUPIDITY, would make me get rid of everything but the dumbbells?" The answer is *afterburn*. The technical name is ***Excess post-exercise oxygen consumption*** (EPOC). It is real. It means the body, yours and mine, keeps burning excess calories following intense exercise that is short in duration. Precisely. Short in duration, meaning minutes. All we need is a spark, and our body takes care of the rest. Provided we eat sensibly and strategically, we get the results we want, while exercising for only a fraction of the time we are used to spending in the gym.

Sound like another type of workout? Yes, I am aware of other formats similar to ours. And we are very different. VERY! It gets even better. **ANABO** has several fitness levels to accommodate a wide range of people. We have varying intensities within each fit level. There is a different pool of exercises specific to each fit level. Again, the workouts are tailored for the individual, meeting them at their individual fitness level. At **ANABO,** we focus on the details.

To achieve results, we must be driven. Therefore, mediocrity is not a game-changer. Mediocrity is a game-killer. Why my client could not "get this weight off," is because he was not driven. His willingness to change was mediocre. He was not sick and tired of being sick and tired of being fat. Only when a person is finally sick and tired of being sick and tired will they make a change? Then, they will be driven to do whatever it takes.

For me, I was not really bodybuilding until I stopped pretending and started training with Al Walke at Flex Gym. I was not setting myself apart from the rest of the world and traditional exercise habits until I cleared out copycat machines, making way for **ANABO**. Yes, although I was spiritually shipwrecked, I won my first Mr. Virginia title in 1999 because I was driven, albeit negatively. My team and I are on the cusp of completing the first **ANABO APP,** partly because we are talented but mostly because we are driven. A number of years would pass before I would ultimately "GO ALL IN" and finally see the Light. This does not have to be your path. If you are a pretender, then stop. Do right. Be right. Act right. Live right. If you are straddling the fence, then pick a side, "GO ALL IN," pray and stay driven.

Chapter Ten: Unstoppable!

"I know that you can do everything and that your plans are unstoppable."
Job 42:2

We are our own biggest obstacle. The only thing stopping us from getting here to there is ourselves. Why? Because, but for ourselves, we are unstoppable. This is factual because God is inside of us. If God is for us, then who or what, anywhere, anytime, can be against us? Nobody, EVER.

In 2001, I was preparing for my second Mr. Virginia competition in 3 years. It was required by the National Physique Committee (NPC) that we qualify in our state every 2 years, so I chose our Virginia state competition to be compliant. I do not remember who won it in 2000, and it did not matter. Whoever was up on stage with me this time was in trouble. Along with my focus and mindset, my body had matured a lot since I won it in 1999, the night I received a standing ovation. This go-round was unique. This time, I was not competing against just some other bodybuilders in Virginia. This time, I was competing against my friend, Big E. He was HUGE. As big as he was, he really was not known for his size. His strength was absolutely insane. That is what we all gawked at him about. He was the strongest dude in the gym, and he was really humble about it.

Big E and I never hung out. Just gym buddies at Flex. The only other place I ever saw him was at one of my old hangouts, Septembers. That place was jumping every Friday and Saturday night. A guy named T-Rex owned it. Ex-NFL player. Big E was a bouncer in Septembers.

One night, I was there with one of my Navy buddies, Larry. We knew each other from Rhode Island. We went to Surface Warfare Officer's School together in Newport, RI. Larry was nuts. He was from Staten Island, NY. Major, major attitude. But we got along really well. Probably because we liked to drink alcohol, and we both had really bad tempers. My normal practice was three to six Honey Brown Lagers from 7-Eleven, then chase it with Jack and Cokes, plural, at the bar. Then, I was set.

On a wild and crowded night at Septembers, Larry and I were drinking and shooting pool. This guy we did not know got an attitude over the pool game. He got in my face and started running his mouth, telling me what he was going to do and blah blah blah. He and I were face to face. Every time I took a sip of my beer, I bumped the tip of his nose with the bottom of my beer bottle. This went on for a few minutes. Meanwhile, Larry, smiling, was standing right behind him with a pool stick in his hand turned upside down. This dude had no idea what was about to happen to him. But guess who did? Big E. He comes rumbling over, breaks it up, grabs the guy, tells me and Larry to settle down, or we had to leave. We played nice. We ended up staying. For the life of me, I still don't know how Big E saw what was about to happen. There was a sea of people in Septembers, dimmed lights, and the music was thumping. Somehow, he sniffed it out. That was probably a good thing. I saw Big E at Flex on Monday. He just shook his head as he passed me.

Me: WHAT? Dude is poppin' off at the mouth about to get his feelings hurt. He never saw it coming.

Big E: I saw the whole thing. It was about to get ugly.

Me: No doubt.

All of this was a distant memory once we started training for the State title. I stopped hanging out at Septembers. I stopped hanging out, period. Once in contest mode, I was locked in. No alcohol, fast food, pizza (my favorite food), sodas, none of a lot of stuff. Things became different between me and Big E at the gym. The imaginary line had been drawn. No friction. No stress. Nothing out of the ordinary. Basically, a quiet mutual respect. Big Al was strategic and careful not to have us practice posing for him in front of one another. Respect.

Now, the rest of the gym was a different story. The line was apparent, and a number of guys picked sides. It felt like half of the gym was for him, and the other half was for me. I was still battling the never-ending, "he is the outsider, he is not from here, he is not from this area," attitude. I do not know if it was as bad as I perceived it to be, or all in my head. Either way, it messed with me. I always felt like I had something to prove. The chip never left my shoulder. I felt like I was under a microscope. If I did something wrong, then EVERYBODY HEARD ABOUT IT. If I did something right, then everybody heard about it.

Sometimes I wore my Walkman, (we did not have Air pods back then) while I trained so I could zone out and not hear the BS. A couple of times, I turned the volume down really low so I could hear what certain people were saying. Clandestine.

Hater: No way, bro. Big E is huge. Look how thick he is. Billy cannot mess with that. Bodzilla, my butt. I got Big E on this one.

Whenever someone questioned my ability, I took it personally. Don't tell me I cannot do something. That is never a good idea. That is the stuff that fires me up. Then I go in deep. Into the darkness. Into the abyss. I use that as fuel. He was Big E. Me? I was Bodzilla! Big E was crazy strong and thick from head to toe. Bodzilla was strong, too. Not as thick, but his shape, little joints, and conditioning were monstrous.

For sixteen weeks, Big E and Bodzilla trained in the same space separately, earnestly, respectfully, and violently. Bodzilla's split was chest, shoulders, and triceps on Mondays. Back, traps, and biceps on Wednesdays. And legs, lower back, and calves on Fridays. He usually threw up after his leg workouts. It was just part of the process. It was not pretty, but it was effective. And it worked.

Of course, Big E and I were not the only ones competing in this competition. We had several competing from Flex Gym. We were a force to be reckoned with. We dominated.

Well, show time was rapidly approaching. We were 3 days out from the competition. My dehydration process was starting to take its toll. I was sitting on the couch at Flex across from the counter. I was in and out of sleep. Al yelled at me,

Al: Hey! What the hell is wrong with you? You alright?

Me: Yeah, I'm good. In and out, really.

Al: Did you take something?

Me: Yeah, trying to dry out. I started taking some new stuff. I am just really hot.

Al: Are you crazy? You are burning up inside! Cut that crap out!

Me: Al, I gotta be ready. These cats are coming for me, man. I gotta be tight.

Al: Fool! YOU WANNA DIE? Cut it out, damnit! I mean it."

Me: Alright. Alright. I am 3 days out.

Al: Pull your shirt up!

That was Al. He was firm. He was direct. He was right! I pulled my shirt up and flexed my abs for him in the mirror. "That's not tight, dummy? Damnit, you are ready right now! Cut it out! I mean it, Ball!"

He always called me Ball. I have no idea why. I never asked. Ha. Al could pretty much call you whatever he wanted and get away with it. I was either Ball or Billy Ball. Either way, I was alright with it.

Two of my boys were at the competition fired up!

Huff: Too big! I see you, boy!

Sid: Rare form, dawg! Rare form! They ain't ready for you. Go ahead and give that man his trophy so he can eat and go home!

The crowd was amped up at the prejudging, which takes place in the daytime. The judges evaluate, critique, and compare the competitors. This is where the contest is won or lost. The night show, which occurs later that evening, is really designed for the audience. By the time the crowd shows up, the judges have already made their decision.

Big E and I stood side by side at center stage. Pumped! Flexed! Tight! Ready! The head judge, Peter Potter, gave his commands,

Head Judge: Quarter turn right. (We turn) Quarter turn right. (We turn) Quarter turn right. (We turn) Quarter turn right. (We turn)

Head Judge: Front double biceps. (Crowd went crazy!) Relax.

Mr. Potter led us through the rest of our mandatories. There was a lot of hooting and hollering. It was exciting. It is what we both trained so hard for. Honestly, it was not even close. I was dialed in. Big E gave me a huge compliment when we got backstage.

Big E: Congrats bro. You rocked it. If it were anybody else, I would not come back tonight. But, out of respect for you, I will be back for the night show.

Me: Thanks, E! I appreciate that man. Nice job today.

That was huge. A lot of competitors do not return for the evening show because they already know the outcome. It meant a lot to me that Big E came back that night. That was a really big deal. That was a tall order. At the night show, I was finally able to settle down, let loose, and put on a show. I was ready to do damage. BODZILLA WENT OFF! Another crowd-pleasing performance. Mr. Virginia, once again!

That was a really special night. My hopes at the time were to continue improving my physique and rising higher on the national level, but that did not happen. As you know, I eventually left Flex a few years later and eventually opened my own gym. Once again, I faced someone who said I could not do what I set out to accomplish. He said there was no money in the gym business, and I would not make it. This man drove all the way from South Orange, New Jersey, six hours away, to try and take the air out of my balloon. He told me that he spoke to a good friend of his who was in the FBI. That is correct. The Federal Bureau of Investigation. He arranged an interview for me with his FBI buddy. This man was my dad.

Was I hurt? No, I was not hurt. I was disgusted! My dad could be loving and supportive, yes. But he could also be terse and critical. This was one of those moments. History showed we did not have the best relationship. We had our differences. He wanted me to continue playing on the tennis team in my final year at Landon. I chose lacrosse. He wanted me to continue playing tennis in college. I chose football. He wanted me to attend the Air Force Academy. I chose the Naval Academy. Roger Yancey was a retired Master Sergeant in the United States Air Force. He was a pilot. He fought in the Vietnam War. He flew Air Force 1 for President Jimmy Carter. He adopted me as his legal son in 1982. I was William Edward Manning Jr for 12 years. When the ink dried, I was William Manning Yancey. He was not my biological father, but he had been part of my life since I was a child. I am eternally grateful for him, nonetheless.

Reflectively, my dad was right. There is no money in the gym business. So, I decided to create a fitness technology company and build an app that people of all ages all over the world can use, exercise for minutes at their own pace and get results. Thanks, Dad! God bless your soul.

You know what? Drew, the muscle head was right, too. I am not a bodybuilder. I am the two-time Mr. Virginia Bodybuilding

Champion. I earned a standing ovation at my first title. The second championship was in defiance of my foes and proof to myself that I was unstoppable. Another crowd-pleasing performance. Thanks, Drew!

My naysayers are consistently wrong. They underestimate me, look around for me on ground level, cannot find me, happen to look up, and well, well, well, there I am again, on another level. Thanks, naysayers! Keep up the good work. You have been bringing me business for years.

My friends, if you are experiencing similar challenges, embrace your naysayers. Many feel compelled to say something hurtful or demeaning, so let them say it. Tell them to keep talking. You are chewing on their words. Success is tasty. You are unstoppable. God says so!

"But I tell you, love your enemies and pray for those who persecute you, that you may be children of your Father in heaven. He causes his sun to rise on the evil and the good and sends rain on the righteous and the unrighteous… Be perfect, therefore, as your heavenly Father is perfect." Matthew 5: 44-48

Chapter Eleven: What's Your Why?

"For I know the plans I have for you," declares the LORD, "plans to prosper you and not to harm you, plans to give you hope and a future."
Jeremiah 29:11

Finally! I realize my purpose. I am here to implore you to be the best version of yourself. A good model would be my son, William, and definitely not the version that I became and was for years. William is the version of me, not tainted by the world. Untransformed. William is love. William is God personified. As a matter of fact, God has been trying to get through to me for a very long time, but I refused to listen. Ignored, ignored, ignored. Ultimately, He began teaching me lessons through William. The most important was, at William's birth, faith.

Today, I stand proudly before you, faithfully. I have a message for you. I am here to relay, communicate, and translate these very lessons to you. I received a fifteen-year crash course to help explain and provide context for the 55 years that I have been on this earth. Here, I have been praying for the fruits of the Spirit for years, and I have had them all along, literally at my fingertips, in William. He exemplifies "love, joy, peace, patience, kindness, goodness, gentleness, faithfulness, and self-control" from Galatians 5:22-23. I recite these every day, several times each day, when all I had to do was look at William.

Every morning, William and I have calls and responses. I start:

Me: I love you

William: I love you

Me: How do we roll?

William: Not if, but when.

Me: Discipline

William: Dominates

Me: No discipline

William: No domination

Me: I fear

William: Nothing. Now faith!

Me: As a man thinketh

William: So is he

Me: Many

William: Mansions

Me: Manners

William: Matter

Me: Don't be

William: Nosy

Me: The truth

William: Is undefeated.

Me: It is

William: Done

Me: It is

William: FINISHED!

As I feed nuggets of God's word to William daily and have him recite them, God is cleverly passing the manna on to me: I love you, not if-but when, be disciplined, fear nothing, have faith, think positively, have good manners, there is a place for me in heaven, don't be nosy, the truth is undefeated, it is finished). All that I was teaching William, God was teaching me. Imparting His wisdom and nourishing me with the fruits of the Spirit:

Lesson I, *LOVE*. Love always wins even when we would rather not, love anyway! Be compassionate and forgive. Forgiving does not mean forgetting. Forgiving means looking past the bitterness and disappointment for the blessing. That is love. It is not easy, but the blessing is for us.

Lesson II, *JOY*. Every day is not promised, but it's joyful to wake up. Each day we are alive is a gift from God. Some days seem longer than others, but prayer works. Joy!

Lesson III, *be PEACEful*. With peace comes serenity. When we are at peace, we are in a state of calm. Calm can be calming to those around us. Start from the inside. Work your way out.

Lesson IV, have *PATIENCE*. Everything happens the way it is supposed to, how it is supposed to, when it is supposed to. God is always on time.

Lesson V, *KINDNESS*. We are so much more credible when we exude kindness and share it with others. Kindness begets kindness. We get what we emit.

Lesson VI, *GOODNESS*. Goodness rejects sin. Goodness evokes positivity. Goodness is God-like.

Lesson VII, *GENTLENESS*. Listening is caring. Caring is listening. A good listener speaks gentleness.

Lesson VIII, *FAITH*. Faith is believing when common sense says not to. When William was born, common sense said to give up on him. We chose not to. Thank God we are uncommon.

Lesson IX, *SELF-CONTROL*. Temptation is always among us. Practice restraint.

William embodies these fruits of the Spirit. He taught me lessons I could never get from Landon, NAPS, the Naval Academy, Flex, Golds, September's, relationships, athletic fields, tennis courts, tracks, teachers, or coaches. The most valuable lessons are not always taught but experienced. Learning can be a conundrum, so God sends us tools. Tools help us navigate our path when we stray away from the intended course. Tools are any instrument used to complete a task: friends, family, work, books, scripture, music, cars, bikes, pens, pencils, computers, you name it. Anything! Quite often, we receive tools along the way and dispose of them or ignore them rather than use them. Choose wisely.

It took me a long time to figure out my "why," my purpose in life. It took years of making mistakes, making poor decisions, and hitting rock bottom, to finally stop digging a hole, then climbing out. It was not until I started climbing that my "why" was realized. Today, I am no longer climbing out of a hole. I am on level ground. The old me is behind me. The old me is a distant memory. The present me is the version of Billy that God intended me to be. I am grateful for His Grace and am happy to share these nuggets of wisdom with all of you.

Do you know "what your why" is? What is your purpose in life? If it's not bigger than you, then it is probably not your "why." If everyone agrees with your "why," then it is probably not really your why. "Whys" do not just have friendlies. "Whys" have foes and oppositions. "Whys" stir up conversations, emotions, and attitudes. 'Whys" make people ask why. I challenge you to find your why. It might surprise you.

"Do not conform to the pattern of this world but be transformed by the renewing of your mind. Then you will be able to test and approve what God's will is-his good, pleasing and perfect will." - Romans 12:2 NIV.

Chapter Twelve: Your Power!

"For God hath not given us the spirit of fear; but of power, and of love, and of a sound mind."
2 Timothy 1:7

One of the most challenging classes for me at the Naval Academy was Chemistry, "the scientific study of the properties and behavior of matter." I believe it takes a specific type of thought processing to embrace, understand, and thrive in this subject. One must be driven! Sadly, I was on the struggle bus. But for one of my greatest mentors, Professor Samuel P. Massie, my Chemistry teacher, I would still be stuck on the side of the road in that dreadful struggle bus. Professor Massie had that specific type of thought processing and thrived in chemistry for years. After all, he helped develop atomic bombs in World War II. He was one of the African-American scientists and technicians on the Manhattan Project. Professor Massie was the first African-American professor at the Naval Academy. He started there two years before I was born, 1966. This was my chemistry teacher. Far be it from me to question him. Professor Massie was not very tall but heavy set. Greying hair and mustache. Slow in his walk, but he got there. Aged, but his wit was quick. Wise, direct, and refined in his teachings and conversation.

Professor Massie: Did you complete the assignment, Mr. Yancey?

Me: Professor Massie, I did my best, sir. It is hard to wrap my head around this stuff. I do not know why all of this is even necessary.

Professor Massie: Ours is not to reason why; ours is but to do and die. Complete the material, Mr. Yancey.

The throes of chemistry alone were challenging enough for me.

Now philosophy?

Me: Yessir, Professor Massie.

In other words, "why" is irrelevant. Do the work. Assessing "why" is not going to make me learn it any faster or easier. The architects of our curriculum, Dr. Massie being one of them, were probably pretty sure of themselves when creating this years ago. Hey, if you are called to assist in the Manhattan Project, then you probably know what the heck you are talking about.

But Professor Massie's response was more profound than the words spoken. In life, how many times have we questioned "why"? How many times have we questioned ourselves? Questioning can shed an assortment of perspectives. Questioning from others can stop us dead in our tracks, at any age.

One day, I had the opportunity to have a conversation with a young person. She was 12 years old. We will call her Jordie. Amazingly coy but tenaciously bright and full of love, vigor, and life. We talked about something that happened at her school. One of her classmates told her she could not do something, and it really bothered her. I leaned down and told her,

Me: Do not ever let anyone take your power. Do you understand? (She gazed up at her mom bewildered, then back at me) If you want to be the best equestrian, then you do it. Do not ever let anyone steal your joy; take your power. Your power is yours to keep, and people will try to take it. Do not ever give it away. Got it?

Jordie: Uh huh (Sheepishly looking up to her mom)

The next time I saw Jordie, I asked if she remembered our little talk about power, and she said yes. As a reminder, I had the word "power" framed along with the definition and gifted it to her.

*"**Never give away your power. Do not let others change the way you think. Remain resolute. Unwavering!**"* Jordie really liked her gift.

A few weeks passed, and her mom shared with me what Jordie was chanting at home one day. "I AM NOT GIVING UP MY POWER! I AM NOT GIVING UP MY POWER!" If we are not careful, our power can escape us without even knowing it, taken or volunteered. It is up to us to keep it protected and tucked away.

I was elected President of the Black Studies Club when I was a junior at the Naval Academy. It was definitely an honor to serve and lead our African-American brothers and sisters, other Midshipmen of color, as well as a few Caucasians. My leadership role had its benefits and responsibilities, of course, but it was also stressful. At that time, in the 90's, the percentage of Black or African Americans was, like today, around 7%. Numerous times, I was asked, "Why do you guys have a Black Studies Club? You trying to take over? We should have a white studies club, don't you think?"

WOW! Was this an attempt to steal my power? Probably, but I think they were also demeaning intentionally. Honestly, at times, I felt like we were targets. As the president, I felt targeted by some, but especially vulnerable because of my position.

Implying there should be a white studies club was passive-aggressive at best and beyond offensive that he would even say it. But these behaviors existed at different levels, even at the top. During one of our Navy home football games, we needed our Brigade of Midshipman, who sat right behind our benches, to cheer louder. It was the second quarter, the game was close, and we needed a boost. A fellow African-American teammate and I grabbed towels, stood up on the bench, turned to face the Brigade, and started waving them to get them fired up. It was all in good spirit. The first half ended, and we headed into the locker room.

Halftime is a time to rest, regroup, address injuries, strategize with our position coach, and then collaborate as a team before returning to the field for the second half. At the Naval Academy, it is not unusual for alumni, Roger Staubach, for instance, to drop in to give words of encouragement. However, it is unusual for a high-ranking administrator to come down from his or her stadium skybox during halftime to speak to the team. This really happened. He was speaking to two players specifically, me and my teammate. He said, "I do not want to see anybody from this football team waving towels at the Brigade. Your heads should be in the game." My fellow towel waver, and I looked at each other befuddled. It seemed that flexing one's power was part of the culture.

Did we stop waving towels at the Brigade of Midshipmen? Yes, we did that day. Did we stop playing aggressively? No! Not even close. We were more aggressive. We were angry! It is one thing to be admonished by your coach. It is another to be berated by a superior. Despite our disappointment, we were vigilant in our efforts to be heard, to stay relevant, and to continue to be a force on the football field and on campus.

That was thirty years ago. From a distance, it appears that a lot of positive change has taken place at my Alma Mater. Nevertheless, there are certain things that I will never forget. One incident in particular did not involve me directly, but it affected me and my African-American classmates and teammates. During one of the meals in King Hall, the dining facility for the Brigade, the professional topic of the week was the "A-6 Intruder," and a Plebe was asked what the initials BN stood for. It is common practice for Plebes to be questioned during meals. What was uncommon was the answer volunteered by an upper-class sitting at the table. "Boat Nigger" is what he said. This spread through the Brigade like wildfire! The term BN actually stands for Bombardier/Navigator, who copilots the A-6 Intruder.

My teammate, Big Mike, shared a room with a guy named Sean. We were all hanging out in their room when the news hit. Once Sean heard who said it, he said, "Ah hell nah! I'm fittin' to kick his butt right now!" He darted out of the room, and I sprinted down the hall to catch him. Fortunately, for all parties, I caught Sean. That could have really gotten out of hand.

"Let me go, Yance! Let me go! I'm sick of this BS!" It took both me and Big Mike to get him back to their room and settle down. It turned out that a number of my teammates were disciplined for verbal threats and looks of intimidation, while the prejudiced, foul-mouthed upperclassman was only verbally reprimanded.

At the Academy, administrators, coaches, teachers, and upperclassmen alike have a major influence. More often than not, their influence is assumed. It becomes a foregone conclusion. This can be problematic because young adults can be grossly misled and mistreated.

It is my understanding that the culture today has vastly improved since we were there. There is increased sensitivity to all races, creeds, colors, and genders. I am grateful for these improvements.

Today, I am blessed to work with hundreds of athletes. It affords me an opportunity to not only strengthen them physically but also mentally, which is of the greatest importance.

My first session with a star football athlete recruited by every Division I program in the country gave me a reason to pause. In light conversation, I picked up on his lack of confidence. I thought to myself, "How can a student-athlete offered a spot on the team of the Head Coach of the #1 college football team in the country lack confidence?" I asked him to rate himself on a scale from one to ten in *strength, talent, speed, and confidence.* His selections were seven, seven, eight, and six, respectively. A SIX IN CONFIDENCE? How is this possible? I had to know, so I asked,

Me: You are one of the best. You are being recruited by every top Division I college football team in the country. On a scale from one to ten, you give yourself a six in self-confidence. HOW IS THIS POSSIBLE?

Athlete: When I was a kid coming up playing little league football, my coach told me to never get too confident. He told me I never knew when I was going to lose. And losing sucks, so don't get my hopes up too high."

Me: SAY WHAT! He told you what!?

Athlete: Yessir. That's what he said.

This is wrong, wrong, wrong, wrong, wrong, wrong, wrong on so many levels. How dare someone drape their own failures and insecurities on another, especially a child?

This is unsettling. You are probably wondering what became of this student-athlete. Well, let us just say the collegiate expectations were never exceeded. Are you surprised?

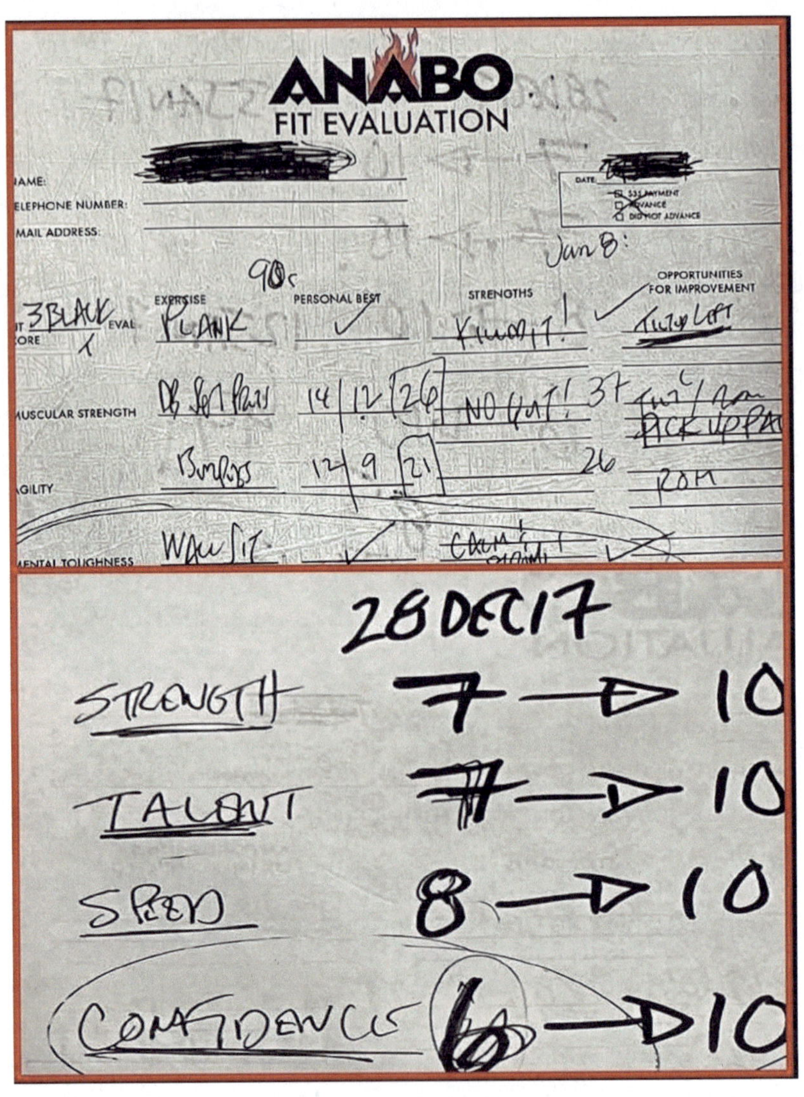

Hurt people can hurt people even when they think they are being helpful. Words can be damaging, life-altering; therefore, picking them wisely is a must. And it's not just the administrators, coaches, and teachers who are culpable. Parents, guardians, friends are responsible as well.

This young man's experience reminded me of Little League football so many years ago. It is amazing how less-than-pleasant happenings hang onto us. I remember my parents discussing my future as the little league quarterback at Danny's Spaghetti House. They both had had enough.

Parents, stand up for your child even if your mom, dad, or guardian did not stand up for you. Unfortunately, our kids do not know any better, which is why they are called kids. Our kids need to be told and then constantly reminded that they are unstoppable, their endeavors are possible, and their dreams are attainable.

There is a **HUGE PURPLE ELEPHANT** in the room that many are either ignoring or knowingly just not putting up a fight. Neither one is acceptable. I have had a number of conversations with parents concerned with "how my child is being led or treated," along with "my child does not want to participate anymore because they say it is no longer fun."

Some common responses to these concerns are, "Well, the coach is just doing his or her job. They are not there to hold hands. Your child needs to toughen up." One, part of the coach's job is to build and manage a positive environment where all participants may learn and excel. Two, I beg your pardon, but the coach is there to metaphorically "hold a child's hand" if need be. In the absence of the parent or guardian, coaches are to fill those shoes posthaste. Thirdly, your "My kid beat up your Honor Role Student" bumper sticker does not work for me. Our kids should not feel intimidated to participate in group or individual activities. "Suck it up, buttercup" is out. "TEAMWORK MAKES THE DREAM WORK" is in!

Some parents are intimidated. They are scared. ITS TIME TO SPEAK UP!

Kids, stand up for yourselves. Stand up for yourself inside yourself. You are **UNSTOPPABLE!** Your endeavors are **POSSIBLE**. Your dreams are **ATTAINABLE**.

Benjamin E. Mays insists, "It isn't a calamity to die with dreams unfulfilled, but it is certainly a calamity not to dream." Young people, your time is now. You are capable. You have the power. I encourage you profusely to never shut down. Whatever the situation, grades, misdemeanor, felony, relationship, fight, pregnancy, depression, sports, classroom, hobby, equestrian, job, ANYTHING, don't keep it all bottled up inside. Talk with someone about it. Talk to your parents, grandparents, cousins, uncle, aunt, guardian, friend, teacher, coach, trainer, SOMEBODY. The last thing you want to do IS NOT TALK ABOUT IT. Do not isolate yourself. That is not an option. Talk to someone, such as a friend, classmate, sibling, parent, grandparent, teacher, or coach. You are not a bad, despicable person who is messed up and cannot be fixed or changed. Everyone makes mistakes. Your mistakes do not define you. This is the furthest from the truth. How you respond is what defines you. We all can change. We all can improve ourselves to be a better version of ourselves, helpful to friends, family, acquaintances, and beyond.

Talk about it. Fellowship heals. When we make a mistake, large or small, it is so easy to think or say to ourselves, "Oh my! What have I done? How could I do this? NO ONE ELSE HAS EVER DONE WHAT I DID. I am so ashamed. No one will ever forgive me. People will talk about me. People will make fun of me. How will I ever overcome this mistake that I made?" Again, the answer is, WE ALL MAKE MISTAKES. Even the people who say they do not make mistakes, DO. If they tell you they do not, then they are lying. It is as simple as that. Listen, you are a good person. You are not a bad person. You are a good person who made a mistake. Learn from the mistake, AND DO NOT REPEAT IT! Remember. Speak up. Do not shut down.

Your body, your mind, and your soul were all God-given. And God always sends help. Be mindful of the tools provided to assist you on your journey. Tools are books, meetings, interviews, exercises, friends, prayers, principals, servicemen, coaches, messages, teammates, firemen, teachers, opportunities, failures, concepts, conversations, doctors, poems, signs, jobs, servers, police officers, recordings, pastors, classmates, bosses, assistants, lawyers, songs, and much more. None of us do it alone. Even you, yourself, can be a tool. God can make anything, anyone, anywhere, anytime a tool. Many are content, leaving them strewn along the road. This is unwise.

Never forget, talent will only get you so far. What elevates you to the next level, propelling you to another orbit, to an even higher stratosphere, is internal. It is "IT'. "IT" is inside you. You cannot see "IT," but you can feel "IT." You will have to dig deep inside yourself. Once found, bask in "IT"! Immerse yourself in "IT." IT is the Holy Spirit! The work you put into your relationship with the Holy Spirit will ignite you. You must commit! The grit, the grind, and the hard work combined with a relentless mindset are all necessary. You must surrender. True submission to the Holy Spirit is paramount. It is the conduit required to free bodies and minds held captive. Go forth, do God's will, and conquer with the Holy Spirit!

Made in the USA
Columbia, SC
18 November 2024

46296941R00074